ON DIALOGUE

On Dialogue is the first comprehensive documentation of the process David Bohm referred to simply as "dialogue." One of the foremost thinkers of the twentieth century, David Bohm continued to refine his notions of dialogue until his death in 1992. This revised and expanded edition of the first booklet of the same name is intended to serve both as a practical working manual for those interested in engaging in dialogue, as well as a theoretical foundation for those who want to probe into the deeper implications of Bohm's dialogical world view.

As conceived by David Bohm, dialogue is a multi-faceted process, looking well beyond conventional ideas of conversational parlance and exchange. It is a process which explores an unusually wide range of human experience: from our closely-held values to the nature and intensity of emotions; the patterns of our thought processes and the function of memory to the manner in which our neurophysiology structures momentary experience. Perhaps most importantly, dialogue explores the manner in which thought – viewed by Bohm as an inherently limited medium, rather than an objective representation of reality – is generated and sustained on a collective level. Such an inquiry necessarily calls into question deeply-held assumptions about culture, meaning, and identity.

David Bohm was Emeritus Professor of Theoretical Physics at Birkbeck College, University of London. Much of his writing is published by Routledge, including *Wholeness and the Implicate Order*, *The Undivided Universe* (with Basil Hiley), *Causality and Chance in Modern Physics*, *Science, Order and Creativity* (with F. David Peat), *Unfolding Meaning*, and *Thought as a System*.

Lee Nichol is a freelance editor and writer, and part of the David Bohm Dialogues group.

proceed by defining a problem we wish to deal with, then systematically apply a solution. But in the realm of relationship, whether inwardly or externally, the posing of a "problem" to be solved creates a fundamentally contradictory structure. Unlike practical problems, where the "thing" to be solved has independence from us (e.g., improving the design of ocean-going vessels), psychological difficulties have no such independence. If I realize that I am susceptible to flattery, and pose this as a problem to be solved, I have made an internal distinction between "myself" and "susceptibility to flattery" which in fact does not exist. Inwardly, I then seem to consist of at least two parts: an urge to believe the flattery, and an urge not to believe the flattery. I am thus proceeding on the basis of a contradiction, which will result in a cycle of confused attempts to "solve" a "problem" whose nature is quite unlike that of a technical problem. Bohm suggests that what is occurring is in fact a *paradox*, not a problem. As a paradox has no discernible solution, a new approach is required, namely, sustained attention to the paradox itself, rather than a determined attempt to eradicate the "problem." From Bohm's perspective, the confusion between problem and paradox operates at all levels of society, from the individual to the global.

"The Observer and the Observed" continues the inquiry into the paradoxical nature of inner experience. Specifically, Bohm addresses the phenomenon of a "central entity," a "self," which observes and acts upon itself. For example, if I see that I am angry, then "I" may try to alter "my anger." At this point, a distinction has occurred: there is the observer – "I," and the observed – "anger." Bohm suggests that this observer is primarily a movement of assumptions and experiences – including anger – but is attributed the status of "entity" through habit, lack of attention, and cultural consensus. This sense of an inner entity carries extremely high value; consequently, a protective mechanism is set in place that allows the "observer" to look both inwardly and outwardly at all variety of "problems," but does not allow sustained consideration of the *nature of the observer itself*. This limitation on the mind's scope of activity is seen to be yet another factor in the generic incoherence of thought.

"Suspension, the Body, and Proprioception" is an exploration of various aspects of awareness that have the potential to cut through the confusion produced by the weight of collective opinion, ill-founded representations, and the illusion of the observer and the observed. Bohm suggests that both on one's own and in the context of a dialogue, it is possible to "suspend" assumptions. For example, if you feel that someone is an idiot, to suspend you would (a) refrain from saying so outwardly and (b) refrain from telling yourself you should not think such things. In this way, the *effects* of the thought, "You are an idiot" (agitation, anger, resentment) are free to run their course, but in a way that allows them to simply be seen, rather than fully identified with. In other words, suspending an assumption or reaction means neither repressing it nor following through on it, but fully attending to it.

In the activity of suspension, the role of the body is of central importance. If a strong impulse is suspended, it will inevitably manifest physically – increased blood pressure, adrenalin, muscular tension, and so on. Likewise, a spectrum of emotions will emerge. In Bohm's view, these components – thoughts, emotions, bodily reactions – are in fact an unbroken whole. However, they sustain one another by appearing to be different – a thought here, a pain in the neck there, and an observer somehow struggling to manage it all. Underlying this activity is a further assumption that the entire difficulty is caused by something "other," something "out there."

Bohm then suggests that "proprioception of thought" may be capable of directly penetrating this cycle of confusion. Physiologically, proprioception provides the body with immediate feedback about its own activity. One can walk up and down steps, for example, without having to consciously direct the body's movement. Further, one can make clear distinctions between what originates within one's body, and what has come from outside. If you move your own arm, you do not have the mistaken impression that someone else has moved it for you. Currently, however, we lack such immediate feedback about the movement of *thought*. Often, therefore, we perceive a difficulty to originate outside ourselves, when in fact it is primarily a construction of thought. Bohm proposes that, with suspension as a basis, the movement of thought can become proprioceptive, much as the body does.

"Participatory Thought and the Unlimited" inquires into the relationship between what Bohm refers to as "literal thought" and "participatory thought." Literal thought is practical and result-oriented, its aim being to form discrete, unequivocal pictures of things "just as they are." Scientific and technical thought are contemporary variants of literal thought.

Bohm suggests that while literal thought has been predominant since the inception of civilization, a more archaic form of perception, formed over the whole of human evolution, remains latent – and at times active – in the structure of our consciousness. This he refers to as "participatory thought," a mode of thought in which discrete boundaries are sensed as permeable, objects have an underlying relationship with one another, and the movement of the perceptible world is sensed as participating in some vital essence. Even today, says Bohm, many tribal cultures maintain aspects of participatory thought.

While acknowledging that such thought is susceptible to projection and error, Bohm nonetheless maintains that at its core, participatory thought is capable of perceiving strata of relationships that are generally inaccessible from a "literal" perspective. Indeed, Bohm suggests that the perspective of participatory thought is not unlike his own vision of the *implicate order*, in which the phenomena of the manifest world are understood as temporary aspects of the movement of a deeper natural order, in a process of perpetual "enfolding" and "unfolding." The essential point to consider, says Bohm, is that both literal thought and participatory thought have virtues and limitations. He makes an appeal for a renewed inquiry into the proper relationship between the two, suggesting that dialogue is uniquely suited to such an exploration.

Finally, Bohm raises doubts as to whether any form of thought can apprehend what he refers to as the "unlimited." As the very nature of thought is to select limited abstractions from the world, it can never really approach the "ground of our being" – that which is unlimited. Yet at the same time, human beings have an intrinsic need to understand and relate to the "cosmic dimension" of existence. To address this apparent disjuncture in our experience, Bohm proposes that *attention*, unlike thought, is potentially unrestricted, and therefore capable of apprehending the subtle nature of the "unlimited."

While the language of such exploration is necessarily metaphorical and inferential, Bohm nonetheless insisted that sustained inquiry into the nature of consciousness and the "ground of being" is essential if we are to have some prospect of bringing an end to fragmentation in the world. It was his firm belief that this fragmentation is rooted in the incoherence of our thought processes, not in immutable laws of nature. He refused to place limitations on where the inquiry into this incoherence may lead, or to draw sharp distinctions between the individual, collective, and cosmic dimensions of humanity. In this respect, dialogue – always a testing ground for the limits of assumed knowledge – offers the possibility of an entirely new order of communication and relationship with ourselves, our fellows, and the world we inhabit.

Lee Nichol
Jemez Springs, New Mexico
November 1995

NOTE

1 David Bohm (1987) *Unfolding Meaning*, London: Routledge, p. 175.

ACKNOWLEDGEMENTS

The editor would like to express his gratitude to Paul and Sherry Hannigan for their good humor, technical support, and commentary in the preparation of the manuscript; to Sarah Bohm, Claudia Krause-Johnson, and Mary Helen Snyder for reading early drafts; to Arleta Griffor for unearthing "On Communication," and to James Brodsky and Phildea Fleming for conceiving the original booklet.

Very special thanks to Sarah Bohm, Arthur Braverman, Theresa Bulla-Richards, Adrian Driscoll, David Moody, and Lynn Powers for their support at critical junctures in the effort to present David Bohm's work to the widest possible reading public.

1

ON COMMUNICATION

During the past few decades, modern technology, with radio, television, air travel, and satellites, has woven a network of communications which puts each part of the world into almost instant contact with all the other parts. Yet, in spite of this world-wide system of linkages, there is, at this very moment, a general feeling that communication is breaking down everywhere, on an unparalleled scale. People living in different nations, with different economic and political systems, are hardly able to talk to each other without fighting. And within any single nation, different social classes and economic and political groups are caught in a similar pattern of inability to understand each other. Indeed, even within each limited group, people are talking of a "generation gap," which is such that older and younger members do not communicate, except perhaps in a superficial way. Moreover, in schools and universities, students tend to feel that their teachers are overwhelming them with a flood of information which they suspect is irrelevant to actual life. And what appears on the radio and television, as well as in the newspapers and magazines, is generally at best a collection of trivial and almost unrelated fragments, while at worst, it can often be a really harmful source of confusion and misinformation.

Because of widespread dissatisfaction with the state of affairs described above, there has been a growing feeling of concern to solve what is now commonly called "the problem of communication." But if one observes efforts to solve this problem, he will notice that different groups who are trying to do this are not actually able to listen to each other. As a result, the very attempt to improve communication leads frequently to yet more

1

confusion, and the consequent sense of frustration inclines people ever further toward aggression and violence, rather than toward mutual understanding and trust.

If one considers the fact that communication is breaking down and that in the present context efforts to prevent this from happening generally tend to accelerate the breakdown, he may perhaps pause in his thinking, to give opportunity to ask whether the difficulty does not originate in some more subtle way that has escaped our mode of formulating what is going wrong. Is it not possible that our crude and insensitive manner of thinking about communication and talking about it is a major factor behind our inability to see what would be an intelligent action that would end the present difficulties?

It may be useful to begin to discuss this question by considering the meaning of the word "communication." This is based on the Latin *commun* and the suffix "ie" which is similar to "fie," in that it means "to make or to do." So one meaning of "to communicate" is "to make something common," i.e., to convey information or knowledge from one person to another in as accurate a way as possible. This meaning is appropriate in a wide range of contexts. Thus, one person may communicate to another a set of directions as to how to carry out a certain operation. Clearly, a great deal of our industry and technology depends on this kind of communication.

Nevertheless, this meaning does not cover all that is signified by communication. For example, consider a dialogue. In such a dialogue, when one person says something, the other person does not in general respond with exactly the same meaning as that seen by the first person. Rather, the meanings are only *similar* and not identical. Thus, when the second person replies, the first person sees a *difference* between what he meant to say and what the other person understood. On considering this difference, he may then be able to see something new, which is relevant both to his own views and to those of the other person. And so it can go back and forth, with the continual emergence of a new content that is common to both participants. Thus, in a dialogue, each person does not attempt to *make common* certain ideas or items of information that are already known to him. Rather, it may be said that the two people are making something *in common*, i.e., creating something new together.

But of course such communication can lead to the creation of something new only if people are able freely to listen to each other, without prejudice, and without trying to influence each other. Each has to be interested primarily in truth and coherence, so that he is ready to drop his old ideas and intentions, and be ready to go on to something different, when this is called for. If, however, two people merely want to convey certain ideas or points of view to each other, as if these were items of information, then they must inevitably fail to meet. For each will hear the other through the screen of his own thoughts, which he tends to maintain and defend, regardless of whether or not they are true or coherent. The result will of course be just the sort of confusion that leads to the insoluble "problem of communication" which has been pointed out and discussed earlier.

Evidently, communication in the sense described above is necessary in all aspects of life. Thus, if people are to co-operate (i.e., literally to "work together") they have to be able to create something in common, something that takes shape in their mutual discussions and actions, rather than something that is conveyed from one person who acts as an authority to the others, who act as passive instruments of this authority.

Even in relationships with inanimate objects and with nature in general, something very like communication is involved. Consider, for example, the work of an artist. Can it properly be said that the artist is *expressing himself*, i.e., literally "pushing outward" something that is already formed inside of him? Such a description is not in fact generally accurate or adequate. Rather, what usually happens is that the first thing the artist does is only *similar* in certain ways to what he may have in mind. As in a conversation between two people, he sees the similarity and the difference, and from this perception something further emerges in his next action. Thus, something new is continually created that is common to the artist and the material on which he is working.

The scientist is engaged in a similar "dialogue" with nature (as well as with his fellow human beings). Thus, when a scientist has an idea, this is tested by observation. When it is found (as generally happens) that what is observed is only similar to what he had in mind and not identical, then from a consideration of the similarities and the differences he gets a new idea which is in turn tested. And so it goes, with the continual emergence of something new that is common to the thought of scientists and what is observed in nature. This extends onward into practical activities, which lead to the creation of new structures that are common to man and to the overall environment in which he lives.

It is clear that if we are to live in harmony with ourselves and with nature, we need to be able to communicate freely in a creative movement in which no one permanently holds to or otherwise defends his own ideas. Why then is it so difficult actually to bring about such communication?

This is a very complex and subtle question. But it may perhaps be said that when one comes to do something (and not merely to talk about it or think about it), one tends to believe that one *already is* listening to the other person in a proper way. It seems then that the main trouble is that the other person is the one who is prejudiced and not listening. After all, it is easy for each one of us to see that other people are "blocked" about certain questions, so that without being aware of it, they are avoiding the confrontation of contradictions in certain ideas that may be extremely dear to them.

The very nature of such a "block" is, however, that it is a kind of insensitivity or "anesthesia" about one's own contradictions. Evidently then, what is crucial is to be aware of the nature of one's own "blocks." If one is alert and attentive, he can see for example that whenever certain questions arise, there are fleeting sensations of fear, which push him away from consideration of these questions, and of pleasure, which attract his thoughts and cause them to be occupied with other questions. So one is able to keep away from whatever it is that he thinks may disturb him. And as a result, he can be subtly defending his own ideas, when he supposes that he is really listening to what other people have to say.

When we come together to talk, or otherwise to act in common, can each one of us be aware of the subtle fear and pleasure sensations that "block" his ability to listen freely? Without this awareness, the injunction to listen to the whole of what is said will have little meaning. But if each one of us can give full attention to what is actually "blocking" communication while he is also attending properly to the content of what is communicated, then we may be able to create something new

4

between us, something of very great significance for bringing to an end the at present insoluble problems of the individual and of society.

2

ON DIALOGUE

The way we start a dialogue group is usually by talking *about* dialogue – talking it over, discussing why we're doing it, what it means, and so forth. I don't think it is wise to start a group before people have gone into all that, at least somewhat. You can, but then you'll have to trust that the group will continue, and that these questions will come out later. So if you are thinking of meeting in a group, one thing which I suggest is to have a discussion or a seminar about dialogue for a while, and those who are interested can then go on to have the dialogue. And you mustn't worry too much whether you are or are not having dialogue – that's one of the blocks. It may be mixed. So we will discuss dialogue for a while – what is its nature?

I give a meaning to the word "dialogue" that is somewhat different from what is commonly used. The derivations of words often help to suggest a deeper meaning. "Dialogue" comes from the Greek word *dialogos*. *Logos* means "the word," or in our case we would think of the "meaning of the word." And *dia* means "through" – it doesn't mean "two." A dialogue can be among any number of people, not just two. Even one person can have a sense of dialogue within himself, if the spirit of the dialogue is present. The picture or image that this derivation suggests is of a *stream of meaning* flowing among and through us and between us. This will make possible a flow of meaning in the whole group, out of which may emerge some new understanding. It's something new, which may not have been in the starting point at all. It's something creative. And this shared meaning is the "glue" or "cement" that holds people and societies together.

Contrast this with the word "discussion," which has the same root as "percussion" and "concussion." It really means to break things up. It emphasizes the idea of analysis, where there may be many points of view, and where everybody is presenting a different one – analyzing and breaking up. That obviously has its value, but it is limited, and it will not get us very far beyond our various points of view. Discussion is almost like a ping-pong game, where people are batting the ideas back and forth and the object of the game is to win or to get points for yourself. Possibly you will take up somebody else's ideas to back up your own – you may agree with some and disagree with others – but the basic point is to win the game. That's very frequently the case in a discussion.

In a dialogue, however, nobody is trying to win. Everybody wins if anybody wins. There is a different sort of spirit to it. In a dialogue, there is no attempt to gain points, or to make your particular view prevail. Rather, whenever any mistake is discovered on the part of anybody, everybody gains. It's a situation called win-win, whereas the other game is win-lose – if I win, you lose. But a dialogue is something more of a common participation, in which we are not playing a game against each other, but *with* each other. In a dialogue, everybody wins.

Clearly, a lot of what is called "dialogue" is not dialogue in the way that I am using the word. For example, people at the United Nations have been having what are often considered to be dialogues, but these are very limited. They are more like discussions – or perhaps trade-offs or negotiations – than dialogues. The people who take part are not really open to questioning their fundamental assumptions. They are trading off minor points, like negotiating whether we have more or fewer nuclear weapons. But the whole question of two different systems is not being seriously discussed. It's taken for granted that you can't talk about *that* – that nothing will ever change that. Consequently their discussions are not serious, not deeply serious. A great deal of what we call "discussion" is not deeply serious, in the sense that there are all sorts of things which are held to be non-negotiable and not touchable, and people don't even want to talk about them. That is part of our trouble.

Now, why do we need dialogue? People have difficulty communicating even in small groups. But in a group of thirty or forty or more, many may find it very hard to communicate unless there is a set purpose, or unless somebody is leading it.

7

Why is that? For one thing, everybody has different assumptions and opinions. They are *basic* assumptions – not merely superficial assumptions – such as assumptions about the meaning of life; about your own self-interest, your country's interest, or your religious interest; about what you really think is important.

And these assumptions are defended when they are challenged. People frequently can't resist defending them, and they tend to defend them with an emotional charge. We'll discuss that in more detail later, but I'll give an example now. We organized a dialogue in Israel a number of years ago. At one stage the people were discussing politics, and somebody said, just in passing, "Zionism is creating a great difficulty in good relations between Jews and Arabs. It is the principal barrier that's in the way." He said it very quietly. Then suddenly somebody else couldn't contain himself and jumped up. He was full of emotion. His blood pressure was high and his eyes were popping out. He said, "Without Zionism the country would fall to pieces!"

That fellow had one basic assumption, and the other person had another one. And those two assumptions were really in conflict. Then the question is, "What can you do?" You see, those are the kinds of assumptions that are causing all the trouble politically, all over the world. And the case I just described is relatively easier than some of the assumptions that we have to handle in politics. The point is that we have all sorts of assumptions, not only about politics or economics or religion, but also about what we think an individual should do, or what life is all about, and so forth.

We could also call these assumptions "opinions." An opinion is an assumption. The word "opinion" is used in several senses. When a doctor has an opinion, that's the best assumption that he can make based on the evidence. He may then say, "Okay, I'm not quite sure, so let's get a second opinion." In that case, if he is a good doctor he does not react to defend his assumption. If the second opinion turns out to be different from his, he doesn't jump up with an emotional charge, such as the fellow did on the question of Zionism, and say, "How can you say such things?" That doctor's opinion would be an example of a rational sort of opinion. But most are not of that nature – mostly they are defended with a strong reaction. In other words, a person identifies himself with them. They are tied up with his investment in self-interest.

The point is that dialogue has to go into all the pressures that are behind our assumptions. It goes into the process of thought *behind* the assumptions, not just the assumptions themselves.

DIALOGUE AND THOUGHT

It is important to see that the different opinions that you have are the result of past thought: all your experiences, what other people have said, and what not. That is all programmed into your memory. You may then identify with those opinions and react to defend them. But it doesn't make sense to do this. If the opinion is right, it doesn't need such a reaction. And if it is wrong, why should you defend it? If you are identified with it, however, you do defend it. It is as if you yourself are under attack when your opinion is challenged. Opinions thus tend to be experienced as "truths," even though they may only be your own assumptions and your own background. You got them from your teacher, your family, or by reading, or in yet some other way. Then for one reason or another you are identified with them, and you defend them.

Dialogue is really aimed at going into the whole thought process and changing the way the thought process occurs collectively. We haven't really paid much attention to thought as a process. We have *engaged* in thoughts, but we have only paid attention to the content, not to the process. Why does thought require attention? Everything requires attention, really. If we ran machines without paying attention to them, they would break down. Our thought, too, is a process, and it requires attention, otherwise it's going to go wrong.

I'll try to give some examples of the difficulty in thinking, in thought. One of these difficulties is *fragmentation*, which originates in thought – it is thought which divides everything up. Every division we make is a result of how we think. In actuality, the whole world is shades merging into one. But we select certain things and separate them from others – for convenience, at first. Later we give this separation great importance. We set up separate nations, which is entirely the result of our thinking, and then we begin to give them supreme importance. We also divide religions by thought – separate religions are entirely a result of how we think. And in the family, the divisions are in thought. The whole way the family is set up is due to the way we think about it.

Fragmentation is one of the difficulties of thought, but there is a deeper root, which is that thought is very active, but the process of thought thinks that it is doing nothing – that it is just telling you the way things are. Almost everything around us has been determined by thought – all the buildings, factories, farms, roads, schools, nations, science, technology, religion – whatever you care to mention. The whole ecological problem is due to thought, because we have thought that the world is there for us to exploit, that it is infinite, and so no matter what we did, the pollution would all get dissolved away.

When we see a "problem," whether pollution, carbon dioxide, or whatever, we then say, "We have got to solve that problem." But we are constantly *producing* that sort of problem – not just that particular problem, but that sort of problem – by the way we go on with our thought. If we keep on thinking that the world is there solely for our convenience, then we are going to exploit it in some other way, and we are going to make another problem somewhere. We may clear up the pollution, but may then create some other difficulty, such as economic chaos, if we don't do it right. We might set up genetic engineering, but if ordinary technology can produce such vast difficulties, imagine the kind of thing genetic engineering could get us into – if we go on with the same way of thinking. People will be doing genetic engineering for whatever suits their fancy and the way they think.

The point is: thought produces results, but thought says it didn't do it. And that is a problem. The trouble is that some of those results that thought produces are considered to be very important and valuable. Thought produced the nation, and it says that the nation has an extremely high value, a supreme value, which overrides almost everything else. The same may be said about religion. Therefore, freedom of thought is interfered with, because if the nation has high value it is necessary to continue to think that the nation has high value. Therefore you've got to create a pressure to think that way. You've got to have an impulse, and make sure everybody has got the impulse, to go on thinking that way about his nation, his religion, his family, or whatever it is that he gives high value. He's got to defend it.

You cannot defend something without first *thinking the defense.* There are those thoughts which might question the thing you want to defend, and you've got to push them aside. That may readily involve self-deception – you will simply push aside a lot of things you would rather not accept by saying they are wrong, by distorting the issue, and so on. Thought defends its basic assumptions against evidence that they may be wrong.

In order to deal with this, we have got to look at thought, because the problem is originating in thought. Usually when you have a problem, you say, "I must think about it to solve it." But what I'm trying to say is that *thought is the problem.* What, therefore, are we going to do? We could consider two kinds of thought – individual and collective. Individually I can think of various things, but a great deal of thought is what we do together. In fact, most of it comes from the collective background. Language is collective. Most of our basic assumptions come from our society, including all our assumptions about how society works, about what sort of person we are supposed to be, and about relationships, institutions, and so on. Therefore we need to pay attention to thought both individually and collectively.

In a dialogue, people coming from different backgrounds typically have different basic assumptions and opinions. In almost any group you will probably find a great many different assumptions and opinions of which we are not aware at the moment. It is a matter of culture. In the overall culture there are vast numbers of opinions and assumptions which help make up that culture. And there are also sub-cultures that are somewhat different from one another according to ethnic groups, or to economic situations, or to race, religion, or thousands of other things. People will come to such a gathering from somewhat different cultures or sub-cultures, with different assumptions and opinions. And they may not realize it, but they have some tendency to defend their assumptions and opinions reactively against evidence that they are not right, or simply a similar tendency to defend them against somebody who has another opinion.

If we defend opinions in this way, we are not going to be able to have a dialogue. And we are often *unconsciously* defending our opinions. We don't usually do it on purpose. At times we may be conscious that we are defending them, but mostly we are not. We just feel that something is so true that we can't avoid trying to convince this stupid person how wrong he is to disagree with us.

Now, that seems the most natural thing in the world – it seems that that's inevitable. Yet if you think of it, we can't really organize a good society if we go on that basis. That's the way democracy is supposed to work, but it hasn't. If everybody has a different opinion, it will be merely a struggle of opinions. And the one who is the strongest will win. It may not necessarily be the right one; it may be that none of them are right. Therefore, we won't be doing the right thing when we try to get together.

This problem arises whenever people meet for dialogue, or legislators try to get together, or businessmen try to get together, or whatever. If we all had to do a job together, we would likely find that each one of us would have different opinions and assumptions, and thus we would find it hard to do the job. The temperature could go way up. In fact, there are people facing this problem in large corporations. The top executives may all have different opinions, hence they can't get together. So the company doesn't work efficiently, it starts to lose money and goes under.

There are some people who are trying to form groups where top business executives can talk together. If politicians would do that, it would be very good. Religious people would be the hardest to get together. The assumptions of the different religions are so firmly embedded that I don't know of any case of two religions, or even sub-groups of any given religion, where they ever got together once they had split. The Christian church, for instance, has been talking about trying to get together for ages and it stays about the same all the time. They talk and they appear to get a little bit closer, and then it never happens. They talk about unity and oneness and love, and all that, but the other assumptions are more powerful; they are programmed into us. Some religious people are trying to get together; they are really sincere – they are as serious as they can be – but it seems that they cannot do it.

Scientists also get into the same situation. Each one may hold to a different view of the truth, so they can't get together. Or they may have different self-interests. A scientist who is working for a company that produces pollution may have a certain self-interest in proving that the pollution is not dangerous. And somebody else might have self-interest in proving that it *is* dangerous. And perhaps then somewhere there is an unbiased scientist who tries to judge it all.

Science is supposed to be dedicated to truth and fact, and religion is supposed to be dedicated to another kind of truth, and to love. But people's self-interest and assumptions take over. Now, we're not trying to judge these people. Something is happening, which is that assumptions or opinions are like computer programs in people's minds. Those programs take over against the best of intentions – they produce their own intentions.

We could say, then, that a group of about twenty to forty people is almost a microcosm of the whole society – like the groups we have just looked at, it has a lot of different opinions and assumptions. It is possible to have a dialogue with one person or with two, three, or four, or you can have the attitude of the dialogue by yourself, as you weigh all the opinions without deciding. But a group that is too small doesn't work very well. If five or six people get together, they can usually adjust to each other so that they don't say the things that upset each other – they get a "cozy adjustment." People can easily be very polite to each other and avoid the issues that may cause trouble. And if there *is* a confrontation between two or more people in such a small group, it seems very hard to stop it; it gets stuck. In a larger group, we may well start out politely. After a while, though, people can seldom continue to avoid all the issues that would be troublesome. The politeness falls away pretty soon. In a group of less than about twenty it may not, because people get to know each other and know the rough edges that they have to avoid. They can take it all into account; it's not too much. But in a group of forty or fifty it *is* too much.

So when you raise the number to about twenty, something different begins to happen. And forty people is about as many as you can conveniently arrange in a circle – or you might put two circles concentrically. In that size group, you begin to get what may be called a "microculture." You have enough people coming in from different sub-cultures so that they are a sort of microcosm of the whole culture. And then the question of culture – the collectively shared meaning – begins to come in.

That is crucial, because the collectively shared meaning is very powerful. The collective thought is more powerful than the individual thought. As we said, the individual thought is mostly the result of collective thought and of interaction with other people. The language is entirely collective, and most of the thoughts in it are. Everybody does his own thing to those thoughts – he makes a contribution. But very few change them very much.

The power of the group goes up much faster than the number of people. I've said elsewhere that it could be compared to a laser. Ordinary light is called "incoherent," which means that it is going in all sorts of directions, and the light waves are not in phase with each other so they don't build up. But a laser produces a very intense beam which *is* coherent. The light waves build up strength because they are all going in the same direction. This beam can do all sorts of things that ordinary light cannot.

Now, you could say that our ordinary thought in society is incoherent – it is going in all sorts of directions, with thoughts conflicting and canceling each other out. But if people were to think together in a coherent way, it would have tremendous power. That's the suggestion. If we have a dialogue situation – a group which has sustained dialogue for quite a while in which people get to know each other, and so on – then we might have such a coherent movement of thought, a coherent movement of communication. It would be coherent not only at the level we recognize, but at the *tacit level*, at the level for which we have only a vague feeling. That would be more important.

"Tacit" means that which is unspoken, which cannot be described – like the knowledge required to ride a bicycle. It is the *actual* knowledge, and it may be coherent or not. I am proposing that thought is actually a subtle tacit process. The concrete process of thinking is very tacit. The meaning is basically tacit. And what we can say explicitly is only a very small part of it. I think we all realize that we do almost everything by this sort of tacit knowledge. Thought is emerging from the tacit ground, and any fundamental change in thought will come from the tacit ground. So if we are communicating at the tacit level, then maybe thought is changing.

The tacit process is common. It is shared. The sharing is not merely the explicit communication and the body language and all that, which are part of it, but there is also a deeper tacit process which is common. I think the whole human race knew this for a million years; and then in five thousand years of civilization we have lost it, because our societies got too big to carry it out. But now we have to get started again, because it has become urgent that we communicate. We have to share our consciousness and to be able to think together, in order to do intelligently whatever is necessary. If we begin to confront what's going on in a dialogue group, we sort of have the nucleus of what's going on in all society. When you are by yourself you miss quite a bit of that; even one-on-one you don't really get it.

ENGAGING IN DIALOGUE

A basic notion for a dialogue would be for people to sit in a circle. Such a geometric arrangement doesn't favor anybody; it allows for direct communication. In principle, the dialogue should work without any leader and without any agenda. Of course, we are used to leaders and agendas, so if we were to start a meeting without a leader – start talking and have no agenda, no purpose – I think we would find a great deal of anxiety in not knowing what to do. Thus, one of the things would be to work through that anxiety, to face it. In fact, we know by experience that if people do this for an hour or two they do get through it and start to talk more freely.

It may be useful to have a facilitator to get the group going, who keeps a watch on it for a while and sort of explains what's happening from time to time, and that kind of thing. But his function is to work himself out of a job. Now, that may take time. It may be that people must meet regularly and sustain the dialogue. That form might be to meet week after week, or bi-weekly or whatever, and sustain it a long time – a year or two or more. In that period, all those things we mentioned would come out. And people would begin to learn really to depend less and less on the facilitator – at least that's the idea behind it. Now, the whole of society has been organized to believe that we can't function without leaders. But maybe we can. That's the suggestion. Of course, it's an experiment. We can't guarantee that it is going to happen. But that is what takes place in any new venture – you consider all the evidence, you consider what's the best idea, what to say about it, what your theories about it are, and then you go ahead and try it.

At the beginning of a dialogue we would not expect that personal problems or questions would enter into it. If people sustained the dialogue week after week, or month after month, then maybe they could. Everything can enter, but the people have to get to know each other and trust each other and establish that relationship of sharing. It would be too much to expect to start with that. And in fact, a personal problem may not be all that important anyway; although if someone has one, the group could consider it. There is no reason why they couldn't; however, I don't think we would begin with that, at least not often. *The group is not mainly for the sake of personal problems; it's mainly a cultural question.* But the personal could come into the group, because personal problems and culture get mixed up.

It is important to understand that a dialogue group is not a therapy group of some kind. We are not trying to cure anybody here, though it may happen as a byproduct. But that's not our purpose. Dr Patrick de Mare, a friend of mine who has gone into this, calls it "socio-therapy," not individual therapy. The group is a microcosm of society, so if the group – or anyone – is "cured," it is the beginning of the larger cure. You can look at it that way if you like. That's limited, but still it's a way to look at it. Nor is this a so-called "encounter group," which is aimed at a particular type of therapy where people's emotions, and so forth, can come up. We are not particularly aiming for that, but we are not saying that emotions should never come up, because in certain cases, if people confront each emotionally it will bring out their assumptions. In the dialogue people should talk directly to one another, one to one, across the circle. Then the time would come, if we got to know each other a bit and could trust each other, when you could speak very directly to the whole group, or to anybody in it.

Some time ago there was an anthropologist who lived for a long while with a North American tribe. It was a small group of about this size. The hunter-gatherers have typically lived in groups of twenty to forty. Agricultural group units are much larger. Now, from time to time that tribe met like this in a circle. They just talked and talked and talked, apparently to no purpose. They made no decisions. There was no leader. And everybody could participate. There may have been wise men or wise women who were listened to a bit more – the older ones – but everybody could talk. The meeting went on, until it finally seemed to stop for no reason at all and the group dispersed. Yet after that, everybody seemed to know what to do, because they understood each other so well. Then they could get together in smaller groups and do something or decide things.

In the dialogue group we are not going to decide what to do about anything. This is crucial. Otherwise we are not free. We must have an empty space where we are not obliged to do anything, nor to come to any conclusions, nor to say anything or not say anything. It's open and free. It's an empty space. The word "leisure" has that meaning of a kind of empty space. "Occupied" is the opposite of leisure; it's full. So we have here a kind of empty space where anything may come in – and after we finish, we just empty it. We are not trying to accumulate anything. That's one of the points about a dialogue. As Krishna-murti used to say, "The cup has to be empty to hold something."

We see that it is not an arbitrary imposition to state that we have no fixed purpose – no absolute purpose, anyway. We may set up relative purposes for investigation, but we are not wedded to a particular purpose, and are not saying that the whole group must conform to that purpose indefinitely. All of us might want the human race to survive, but even that is not our purpose. Our purpose is really to communicate coherently in truth, if you want to call that a purpose.

You could say that generally our culture goes in for large groups of people for two reasons. One is for entertainment and fun. The other is to get a useful job done. Now, I'm going to propose that in a dialogue we are not going to have any agenda, we are not going to try to accomplish any useful thing. As soon as we try to accomplish a useful purpose or goal, we will have an assumption behind it as to what is useful, and that assumption is going to limit us. Different people will think different things are useful. And that's going to cause trouble. We may say, "Do we want to save the world?" or "Do we want to run a school?" or "Do we want to make money?" Whatever it may be. That's also going to be one of the problems in corporate dialogues. Will they ever give up the notion that they are there primarily to make a profit? If they could, this would be a real transformation of mankind. I think that many business executives in certain companies are feeling unhappy and really want to do something – not merely to save the company. Just as we are, they are unhappy about the whole world. It's not that all of them are money-grubbing or exclusively profit-oriented.

When a dialogue group is new, in general people talk around the point for a while. In all human relations nowadays, people generally have a way of not directly facing anything. They talk around things, avoiding the difficulties. This practice will probably continue within a dialogue group. If you keep the group going for a while though, that tendency begins to break down. At a dialogue one evening a fellow spoke up, saying, "Okay, we're all talking about philosophy. Can I read this nice bit of philosophy I brought?" And some people said, "No." So he didn't read it. It seemed a bit of a shock, but it worked out.

It all has to be worked out. People will come to a group with different interests and assumptions. In the beginning they may have negotiation, which is a very preliminary stage of dialogue. In other words, if people have different approaches, they have to negotiate somehow. However, that is not the end of dialogue; it is the beginning. Negotiation involves finding a common way of proceeding. Now, if you only negotiate, you don't get very far – although some questions do have to be negotiated.

A great deal of what nowadays is typically considered to be dialogue tends to focus on negotiation; but as we said, that is a preliminary stage. People are generally not ready to go into the deeper issues when they first have what they consider to be a dialogue. They negotiate, and that's about as far as they get. Negotiation is trading off, adjusting to each other and saying, "Okay, I see your point. I see that that is important to you. Let's find a way that would satisfy both of us. I will give in a little on this, and you give in a little on that. And then we will work something out." Now, that's not really a close relationship, but it begins to make it possible to get going.

So the suggestion is that people could start dialogue groups in various places. The point would not be to identify with the group, but rather, what is important is this whole process. You might say, "This is a wonderful group," but it's actually the process that counts.

I think that when we are able to sustain a dialogue of this sort you will find that there will be a change in the people who are taking part. They themselves would then behave differently, even outside the dialogue. Eventually they would spread it. It's like the Biblical analogy of the seeds – some are dropped in stony ground and some of them fall in the right place and they produce tremendous fruit. The thing is that you cannot tell where or how it can start. The idea here, the communication here, the kind of thought we're having here, is a kind of seed which may help this to come about. But we mustn't be surprised if many of these groups are abortive and don't get going. That doesn't mean it can't happen.

The point is not to establish a fixed dialogue group forever, but rather one that lasts long enough to make a change. If you keep holding it for too long it may become caught up in habits again. But you have to keep it up for a while, or else it won't work. It may be valuable to keep the dialogue going for a year or two, as we said, and it is important to sustain it regularly. If you sustain it, all these problems will arise; it cannot avoid bringing out the deep assumptions of the people who are participating. The frustration will arise, the sense of chaos, the sense that it's not worth it. The emotional charge will come. The fellow with the assumptions about Zionism probably wanted to be very polite. But suddenly somebody said something that outraged him, and he couldn't control himself. It's going to happen that the deep assumptions will come to the surface, if we stick with it. But if you understand that you do nevertheless have to stick with it, then something new will come.

Now, dialogue is not going to be always entertaining, nor is it doing anything visibly useful. So you may tend to drop it as soon as it gets difficult. But I suggest that it is very important to go on with it – to stay with it through the frustration. When you think something is important you will do that. For example, nobody would climb Mount Everest unless for some reason he thought it was important, as that could also be very frustrating and not always entertaining. And the same is true if you have to make money, or do all sorts of things. If you feel that they are necessary, you do them.

I'm saying that it is necessary to share meaning. A society is a link of relationships among people and institutions, so that we can live together. But it only works if we have a *culture* – which implies that we share meaning; i.e., significance, purpose, and value. Otherwise it falls apart. Our society is incoherent, and doesn't do that very well; it hasn't for a long time, if it ever did. The different assumptions that people have are *tacitly* affecting the whole meaning of what we are doing.

SUSPENDING ASSUMPTIONS

We have been saying that people in any group will bring to it their assumptions, and as the group continues meeting, those assumptions will come up. Then what is called for is to *suspend* those assumptions, so that you neither carry them out nor suppress them. You don't believe them, nor do you disbelieve them; you don't judge them as good or bad. Normally when you are angry you start to react outwardly, and you may just say something nasty. Now suppose I try to suspend that reaction. Not only will I now not insult that person outwardly, but I will suspend the insult that I make *inside* of me. Even if I don't insult somebody outwardly, I am insulting him inside. So I will suspend that, too. I hold it back, I reflect it back. You may also think of it as suspended in front of you so that you can look at it – sort of reflected back as if you were in front of a mirror. In this way I can see things that I wouldn't have seen if I had simply carried out that anger, or if I had suppressed it and said, "I'm not angry" or "I shouldn't be angry."

So the whole group now becomes a mirror for each person. The effect you have on the other person is a mirror, and also the effect the other person has on you. Seeing this whole process is very helpful in bringing out what's going on, because you can see that everybody's in the same boat.

What's required then is that we notice the connection between the thoughts going on in the dialogue, the feelings in the body, and the emotions. If you watch, you'll see from the body language, as well as from the verbal language, that everybody's in much the same boat – they're just on opposite sides. The group may even polarize so that two very powerful groups are against each other. But one of the things we're aiming for is that this *should* come out. We're not trying to suppress it.

Therefore, you simply see what the assumptions and reactions mean – not only your own, but the other people's as well. We are not trying to change anybody's opinion. When this meeting is over, somebody may or may not change his opinion. This is part of what I consider dialogue – for people to realize what is on each other's minds without coming to any conclusions or judgments. Assumptions will come up. And if you hear some-body else who has an assumption that seems outrageous to you, the natural response might be to get angry, or get excited, or to react in some other way. But suppose you suspend that activity. You may not even have known that you had an assumption. It was only because he came up with the opposite one that you find out that you have one. You may uncover other assumptions, but we are all suspending them and looking at them all, seeing what they mean.

You have to notice your own reactions of hostility, or what-ever, and you can see by the way people are behaving what their reactions are. You may find, as with anger, that it could go so far that the meeting could blow up. If temperatures do rise, then those who are not completely caught up in their particular opinions should come in to defuse the situation a bit so that people could look at it. It mustn't go so far that you can't look at it. The point is to keep it at a level where the opinions come out, but where you can look at them. Then you may have to see that the other person's hostility provokes your own. That's all part of the observation, the suspension. You become more familiar with how thought works.

THE IMPULSE OF NECESSITY

We've been discussing dialogue and thought, and the import-ance of giving attention to the whole process – not merely to the content of all the different opinions and views – and to how we hold it all together. Also we're all watching the process of how it affects us, our feelings and states of the body, and how other people are affected. This is really something of crucial importance, to be listening and watching, observing, to give attention to the actual process of thought and the order in which it happens, and to watch for its incoherence, where it's not working properly, and so on. *We are not trying to change anything, but just being aware of it. And you can notice the similarity of the difficulties within a group to the conflicts and incoherent thoughts within an individual.*

I think that as we do this we will find that certain kinds of thoughts play a greater role than other kinds. One of the kinds that is most important is the thought of *necessity*. What is neces-sary cannot be otherwise; it's just got to be that way. It is interesting that the word *necessary* has a Latin root, *necesse*, meaning "don't yield." It really means "what cannot be turned aside." Ordinarily as we go through life, problems come up and they can be turned aside, or if they can't be turned aside then *we* turn aside, and that is the way we resolve things. But then there may arise a necessity, as I said, which cannot be turned aside; but we may have our own necessity which also cannot be turned aside. Then we feel frustrated. Each necessity is absolute, and we have a conflict of absolute necessities. Typically, it may come up that your own opinion cannot be turned aside, nor can the other person's, and you feel the other person's opinion working within you, opposing you. So each person is in a state of conflict.

Necessity creates powerful impulses. Once you feel that something is necessary, it creates an impulse to do it or not to do it, whatever it may be. It may be very strong and you feel compelled, propelled. Necessity is one of the most powerful forces – it overrides all the instincts eventually. If people feel something is necessary, they'll even go against the instinct of self-preservation and all sorts of things. In the dialogue, both individually and collectively – this is important – the conflicts come up around this notion of necessity. All the serious arguments, whether in the family or in the dialogue, are about different views of what is *absolutely necessary*. Unless it takes that form, then you can always negotiate it and decide what has first priority, and adjust it. But if two things are absolutely necessary you cannot use the usual way of negotiation. That is the weak point about negotiation. When two different nations come up and each one says, "I'm sovereign, and what I say has to go: it's absolutely necessary," then there is no answer unless they can change that.

The question is what to do if there is a clash of two absolute necessities. The first thing that happens is that we get this emotional charge and we can build up powerful feelings of anger, hate, frustration, as I described before. As long as that absolute necessity remains, nothing can change it, because in a way each person says that they have a valid reason to stick to what they've got, and they have a valid reason to hate the other person for getting in the way of what is absolutely necessary: "He rather obstinately and stupidly refuses to see this," and so on. One may say that it's regrettable that we have to kill all these people, but it is absolutely necessary, in the interests of the country, the religion, or whatever it may be. So you see the power of that notion.

So in the dialogue we are expecting the notions of absolute necessity to come up, to clash with each other. People avoid that, because they know that there's going to be trouble and they skirt those questions. But if we sustain the dialogue it's going to come up. The question is what happens then.

We discussed previously that something can happen, if people will stay with it, which will change their whole attitude. At a certain moment we may have the insight that each one of us is doing the same thing – sticking to the absolute necessity of his idea – and that nothing can happen if we do that. If so, it may raise the question "Is it absolutely necessary? So much is being destroyed just because we have this notion of it being absolutely necessary." Now if you can question it and say, "Is it absolutely necessary?" then at some point it may loosen up. People may say, "Well, maybe it's not absolutely necessary." Then the whole thing becomes easier, and it becomes possible to let that conflict go and to explore new notions of what is necessary, creatively. The dialogue can then enter a creative new area. I think this is crucial.

What about these notions of necessity which we have to set up or discover? If an artist just puts on his paint in arbitrary places, you would say there wasn't anything to it; if he just follows somebody else's order of necessity, he's mediocre. He's got to create his own order of necessity. Different parts of the form he is making must have an inner necessity or else the thing has not really much of a value. This artistic necessity is creative. The artist has his freedom in this creative act. Therefore, freedom makes possible *a creative perception of new orders of necessity*. If you can't do that, you're not really free. You may say you're doing whatever you like and that's your impulse, but I think we've seen that your impulses can come from your thoughts. For example, the thought of what is necessary will make an impulse, and people who are in international conflict will say our impulse is to go to war and get rid of these people who are in our way, as if that were freedom. But it isn't. They're being driven by that thought. So doing what you like is seldom freedom, because what you like is determined by what you think and that is often a pattern which is fixed. Therefore we have a creative necessity which we discover – you can discover individually or we can do so collectively in the group – of how to operate in a group in a new way. Any group which has problems really has got to solve them creatively if they're serious problems. It can't just be by trade-offs and negotiations of the old ways.

I think this is one of the key points, then – to realize when you come to an assumption, that there is an assumption of absolute necessity which you're getting into, and that's why everything is sticking.

PROPRIOCEPTION OF THOUGHT

You can see the whole scope of this question of dialogue giving attention to thought may look rather elementary or simple in the beginning, but it actually gets to the root of our problems and opens the way to creative transformation.

We come back to the realization that the thing which has gone wrong with thought is basically, as I said before, that it does things and then says or implies that it didn't do them – that they took place independently, and that they constitute "problems." Whereas what you really have to do is to stop thinking that way so that you stop creating that problem. The "problem" is insoluble as long as you keep on producing it all the time by your thought. Thought has to be in some sense aware of its consequences, and presently thought is not sufficiently aware of its consequences. That ties up with something similar in neurophysiology called *proprioception*, which really means "self-perception." The body can perceive its own movement. When you move the body you know the relation between intention and action. The impulse to move and the movement are seen to be connected. If you don't have that, the body is not viable.

We know of a woman who apparently had a stroke in the middle of the night. She woke up and she was hitting herself. People came in and turned on the light and that's what they found. What happened was that her motor nerves were working, but her sensory nerves were no longer working. So she probably touched herself, but she didn't know that she'd touched herself, and therefore she assumed that somebody else was touching her and interpreted that as an attack. The more she defended, the worse the attack got. The proprioception had broken down. She no longer saw the relation between the inten-

24

tion to move and the result. When the light was turned on, proprioception was established in a new way, by sight.

The question is: can thought be proprioceptive? You have the intention to think, which you're not usually aware of. You think because you have an intention to think. It comes from the idea that it is necessary to think, that there's a problem. If you watch, you'll see an intention to think, an impulse to think. Then comes the thought, and the thought may give rise to a feeling, which might give rise to another intention to think, and so on. You're not aware of that, so the thought appears as if it were coming by itself, and the feeling appears to be coming by itself, and so on. That gives the wrong meaning, as in the case of the woman we talked about just now. You may get a feeling that you don't like from a thought, and then a second later say, "I've got to get rid of that feeling," but your thought is still there working, especially if it's a thought that you take to be absolutely necessary.

In fact, the problems we have been discussing are basically all due to this lack of proprioception. *The point of suspension is to help make proprioception possible, to create a mirror so that you can see the results of your thought.* You have it inside yourself because your body acts as a mirror and you can see tensions arising in the body. Also other people are a mirror, the group is a mirror. You have to see your intention. You get an impulse to say something and you see it there, the result, at almost the same time.

If everybody is giving attention, then there will arise a new kind of thought between people, or even in the individual, which is proprioceptive, and which doesn't get into the kind of tangle that thought gets into ordinarily, which is not proprioceptive. We could say that practically all the problems of the human race are due to the fact that thought is not proprioceptive. Thought is constantly creating problems that way and then trying to solve them. But as it tries to solve them it makes it worse because it doesn't notice that it's creating them, and the more it thinks, the more problems it creates – because it's not proprioceptive of what it's doing. If your body were that way you would very quickly come to grief and you wouldn't last very long. And it may be said that if our culture were that way, our civilization would not last all that long, either. So this is another way in which dialogue will help collectively to bring about a different kind of consciousness.

COLLECTIVE PARTICIPATION

All of this is part of collective thought – people thinking together. At some stage we would share our opinions without hostility, and we would then be able to *think together*; whereas when we defend an opinion we can't. An example of people thinking together would be that somebody would get an idea, somebody else would take it up, somebody else would add to it. The thought would flow, rather than there being a lot of different people, each trying to persuade or convince the others.

In the beginning, people won't trust each other. But I think that if they see the importance of the dialogue, they will work with it. And as they start to know each other, they begin to trust each other. It may take time. At first you will just come into the group bringing all the problems of the culture and the society. Any group like this is a microcosm of society – it has all sorts of opinions, people not trusting each other, and so on. So you begin to work from there. People talk at first in a perhaps rather trivial way, and then later less trivially. Initially they talk about superficial issues, because they're afraid of doing more, and then gradually they learn to trust each other.

The object of a dialogue is not to analyze things, or to win an argument, or to exchange opinions. Rather, it is to suspend your opinions and to look at the opinions – to listen to everybody's opinions, to suspend them, and to see what all that means. If we can see what all of our opinions mean, then we are *sharing a common content*, even if we don't agree entirely. It may turn out that the opinions are not really very important – they are all assumptions. And if we can see them all, we may then move more creatively in a different direction. We can just simply share the appreciation of the meanings; and out of this whole thing, truth emerges unannounced – not that we have chosen it.

If each of us in this room is suspending, then we are all doing the same thing. We are all looking at everything together. The content of our consciousness is essentially the same. Accordingly, a different kind of consciousness is possible among us, a *participatory consciousness* – as indeed consciousness always is,

26

but one that is frankly acknowledged to be participatory and can go that way freely. Everything can move between us. Each person is participating, is partaking of the whole meaning of the group and also taking part in it. We can call that a true dialogue.

Something more important will happen if we can do this, if we can manage it. Everybody will be sharing all the assumptions in the group. If everybody sees the meaning together, of all the assumptions, then the content of consciousness is essentially the same. Whereas if we all have different assumptions and defend them, each person is then going to have a different content, because we won't really take in the other person's assumptions. We'll be fighting them, or pushing them away – trying to convince or persuade the other person.

Conviction and persuasion are not called for in a dialogue. The word "convince" means to win, and the word "persuade" is similar. It's based on the same root as are "suave" and "sweet." People sometimes try to persuade by sweet talk or to convince by strong talk. Both come to the same thing, though, and neither of them is relevant. There's no point in being persuaded or convinced. That's not really coherent or rational. If something is right, you don't need to be persuaded. If somebody has to persuade you, then there is probably some doubt about it.

If we could all share a common meaning, we would be participating together. We would be partaking of the common meaning – just as people partake of food together. We would be taking part and communicating and creating a common meaning. That would be participation, which means both "to partake of" and "to take part in." It would mean that in this participation a common mind would arise, which nonetheless would not exclude the individual. The individual might hold a separate opinion, but that opinion would then be absorbed into the group, too.

Thus, everybody is quite free. It's not like a mob where the collective mind takes over – not at all. It is something *between* the individual and the collective. It can move between them. It's a harmony of the individual and the collective, in which the whole constantly moves toward coherence. So there is both a collective mind and an individual mind, and like a stream, the flow moves between them. The opinions, therefore, don't matter so much. Eventually we may be somewhere between all these

27

opinions, and we start to move beyond them in another direction – a tangential direction – into something new and creative.

A NEW CULTURE

A society is a link of relationships that are set by people in order to work and live together: rules, laws, institutions, and various things. It is done by thinking and agreeing that we are going to have them, and then we do it. And behind that is a culture, which is shared meaning. Even to say that we want to set up a government, people must agree to a common meaning of what kind of government they want, what's good government, what's right, and so on. Different cultures will produce different functions of government. And if some people don't agree, then we have political struggle. When it goes further, it breaks down into civil war.

I am saying society is based on shared meanings, which constitute the culture. If we don't share coherent meaning, we do not make much of a society. And at present, the society at large has a very incoherent set of meanings. In fact, this set of "shared meanings" is so incoherent that it is hard to say that they have any real meaning at all. There is a certain amount of significance, but it is very limited. The culture in general is incoherent. And we will thus bring with us into the group – or microcosm or microculture – a corresponding incoherence.

If all the meanings can come in together, however, we may be able to work toward coherence. As a result of this process, we may naturally and easily drop a lot of our meanings. But we don't have to begin by accepting or rejecting them. The important thing is that we will never come to truth unless the overall meaning is coherent. All the meanings of the past and the present are together. We first have to apprehend them, and just let them be; and this will bring about a certain order.

If we can work this through, we will then have a coherent meaning in the group, and hence the beginning of a new kind of culture – a culture of a kind which, as far as I can tell, has never really existed. If it ever did, it must have been very long ago – maybe in some groups in the primitive Stone Age conditions. I am saying that a genuine culture could arise in which opinions and assumptions are not defended incoherently.

And that kind of culture is necessary for the society to work, and ultimately for the society to survive.

Such a group might be the germ or the microcosm of the larger culture, which would then spread in many ways – not only by creating new groups, but also by people communicating the notion of what it means.

Also, one can see that it is possible that this spirit of the dialogue can work even in smaller groups, or one-on-one, or within the individual. If the individual can hold all of the meanings together in his own mind, he has the attitude of the dialogue. He could carry that out and perhaps communicate it, both verbally and non-verbally, to other people. In principle, this could spread. Many people are interested in dialogue now. We find it growing. The time seems to be ripe for this notion, and it could perhaps spread in many different areas.

I think that something like this is necessary for society to function properly and for society to survive. Otherwise it will all fall apart. This shared meaning is really the cement that holds society together, and you could say that the present society has some very poor-quality cement. If you make a building with very low-quality cement, it cracks and falls apart. We really need the right cement, the right glue. And that is shared meaning.

DIFFICULTIES IN DIALOGUE

We have talked about the positive side of dialogue. However, this attempt at dialogue can be very frustrating. I say this not only theoretically, but also from experience. We've mentioned some of the difficulties: it's frustrating to have all these opinions; there may be anxiety. Besides that, you will find other problems in trying to have a dialogue in a group of any size. Some people want to assert themselves; that's their way of going about things. They talk easily and they become dominant. They may have an image of themselves as dominant, and they get a certain amount of security out of it, a lift out of it. Other people, however, do not have such great self-esteem in this area; they tend to hold back, especially when they see somebody who is dominant. They are afraid that they'll make fools of themselves, or something of the kind.

There are various roles that people adopt. Some people adopt the dominant role, some adopt the role of the weak, powerless person who can be dominated. They sort of work together, with each other. Those "roles," which are really based on assumptions and opinions, will also interfere with the operation of dialogue. So a person has built some assumptions about himself, whether it's one way or the other. Also, since his childhood people have told him that that's what he is, that he is this way or that way. He has had bad experiences or good experiences, and it all built up. These are some of the problems which will arise when we try to have a dialogue.

A further difficulty is you find that very often there is an impulse or pressure, a compulsion almost, to get in there quickly and get your point of view across, particularly if you are one of the "talkers." Even if you're not, you have that pressure, but you're holding back because you're frightened. Therefore, there is no time for people to absorb what has been said, or to ponder it. People feel under pressure to get in, and people feel left out. The whole communication breaks down for this very elementary reason. This is nothing deep at all, but still we have got to address it. Very often when you don't give space in a group, everybody jumps in right away with whatever he has in his mind. But at the same time, you shouldn't be mulling it over in your mind – picking on one point and turning it over – while the conversation goes on to something else. If you stop to think about one point, by the time you have thought about it the group has moved on, and what you were going to say is now irrelevant. As you were thinking, "What does all that mean and what shall I say about it?" it became too late, because the topic has changed. So there is sort of a subtle situation in between, where you are not jumping in too fast, nor holding back too much. There may be silent periods, and so on.

So while we don't have "rules" for the dialogue, we may learn certain principles as we go along which help us – such as that we must give space for each person to talk. We don't put this as a rule; rather we say that we can see the sense of it, and we are learning to do it. So we see the necessity or value of certain procedures that help.

Also, if someone wants the group to accomplish his idea or purpose, it would probably start a conflict. The dialogue is aimed for those people who can commonly agree that this is the way to go about it. If people don't agree that this is the way to go about it, then there is no reason to be in it. Frequently you find that as the dialogue goes on and the group continues, some people leave and others come in. There are those who feel, "Well, this is not for me."

Now, how are you going to deal with the frustrations within the group? As we said before, things may make you angry or frustrated or may frighten you. Your assumptions may be revealed and challenged, and you may find the opinions of others to be outrageous. Also, people may be frightened and anxious if there is no leader and no topic and nothing "to do." So you have to get through all of that.

These are the problems that are going to arise – that have arisen in all the groups that I've seen. And you can expect that they are almost inevitable, and may ask, "Then what is the point in going on with all of this?" So we must explore that.

THE VISION OF DIALOGUE

Let me give what I call a "vision of dialogue." You don't have to accept it, but it may be a way to look at it. Let's suppose we stick with this, and we face the emotional charge – all this irritation, all this frustration – which actually can develop into hate if very powerful assumptions are there. We could say that hate is a neurophysiological, chemical disturbance of a very powerful kind, which is now endemic in the world. Wherever you look, you see people hating each other. So suppose you stick with this. You may get an insight, a shared insight, that we're all in the same position – everybody has an assumption, everybody is sticking to his assumption, everybody is disturbed neurochemically. The fundamental level in people is the same; the superficial differences are not so important.

It's possible to see that there's a kind of "level of contact" in the group. The thought process is an extension of the body process, and all the body language is showing it, and so on. People are really in rather close contact – hate is an extremely close bond. I remember somebody saying that when people are in really close contact, talking about something which is very important to them, their whole bodies are involved – their hearts, their adrenalin, all the neurochemicals, everything. They are in far closer contact with each other than with some parts of their own bodies, such as their toes. So, in some sense there is established in that contact "one body." And also, if we can

31

all listen to each other's opinions, and suspend them without judging them, and your opinion is on the same basis as anyone else's, then we all have "one mind" because we have the *same content* – all the opinions, all the assumptions. At that moment the difference is secondary. Then you have in some sense one body, one mind. It does not overwhelm the individual. There is no conflict in the fact that the individual does not agree. It's not all that important whether you agree or not. There is no pressure to agree or disagree.

The point is that we would establish, on another level, a kind of bond, which is called impersonal fellowship. You don't have to know each other. In England, for example, the football crowds prefer not to have seats in their football stands, but just to stand bunched against each other. In those crowds very few people know each other, but they still feel something – that contact – which is missing in their ordinary personal relations. And in war many people feel that there's a kind of comradeship which they miss in peacetime. It's the same sort of thing – that close connection, that fellowship, that mutual participation. I think people find this lacking in our society, which glorifies the separate individual. The communists were trying to establish something else, but they completely failed in a very miserable way. Now a lot of them have adopted the same values as we have. But people are not entirely happy with that. They feel isolated. Even those who "succeed" feel isolated, feel there's another side they are missing.

I am saying that this is a *reason* for dialogue. We really do need to have it. This reason should be strong enough to get us through all the frustration we talked about. People generally seem ready to accept frustration with anything that they regard as important. Doing your job or making money, for example, is often frustrating; it produces anxiety. Yet people will say, "That is important! We have to stick with it." They feel that way about all sorts of things. I'm saying that if we regard dialogue as important, as necessary, we will say about it as well, "We will stick to it." But if we don't think it is necessary, we might say, "Okay, what's the point? This is too much trouble. Let's give it up. It's not producing anything." You see, you have to explore anything new for a while. In science, or anywhere, you usually have to go through a period where you are not getting anywhere while you are exploring. It can, nevertheless, be very discouraging.

If we can all suspend carrying out our impulses, suspend our assumptions, and look at them all, then we are all in the same state of consciousness. And therefore we have established the thing that many people say they want – a common consciousness. It may not be very pleasant, but we have got it. People tend to think of common consciousness as "shared bliss." That may come; but if it does, I'm saying that the road to it is through this. We have to share the consciousness that we *actually* have. We can't just impose another one. But if people can share the frustration and share their different contradictory assumptions and share their mutual anger and stay with it – if everybody is angry together, and looking at it together – then you have a common consciousness.

If people could stay with power, violence, hate, or whatever it is, all the way to the end, then it would sort of collapse – because ultimately they would see that we are all the same. And consequently they would have participation and fellowship. People who have gone through that can become good friends. The whole thing goes differently. They become more open and trusting to each other. *They have already gone through the thing that they are afraid of,* so the intelligence can then work.

There's a story I would like to relate in this connection. I knew a man in London who had been a child psychiatrist. He told me that somebody once brought to him a girl about seven years old who was very disturbed. She refused to talk to anybody. They brought her hoping that he would help to get her talking. So he tried for about an hour and got nowhere. Finally, getting exasperated, he said, "Why don't you talk to me?" She answered, "Because I hate you." He thought that he had to bring time into this somewhere to defuse it. So he said, "How long will you hate me?" She said, "I'll hate you forever." He was then a bit worried, so he brought time in again. He asked, "How long will you hate me forever?" Then she burst out laughing and the whole thing was broken. The energy which had been there was now available. The absurdity of the thing was shown to her – that the thing was incoherent. She was saying that she was going to hate him forever, and she could see that that wouldn't really be so; and if that's not so, then the idea that she has got to go on with the hatred is not necessary either.

When you have anger, it has a reason, or a cause. You say that you are angry because of this, this, or that. It builds up to rage and hate, at which point it no longer has a particular reason anymore – it just sustains itself. That energy of hate is sort of locked up, and then it's looking for an occasion to discharge. The same holds with panic. You are usually aware of a reason for your fear, but by the time you get to panic it goes on by itself. However, the sort of energy that goes around at that level may also in a vague way be the kind of energy we are talking about for creativity – namely, *an energy without a reason*.

But there is a great deal of violence in the opinions that we are defending. They are not merely opinions, they are not merely assumptions; they are assumptions with which we are identified – which we are therefore defending, because it is as if we are defending ourselves. The natural self-defense impulse, which we got in the jungle, has been transferred from the jungle animals to these opinions. In other words, we say that there are some dangerous opinions out there – just as there might be dangerous tigers. And there are some very precious animals inside us that have to be defended. So an impulse that made sense physically in the jungle has been transferred to our opinions in our modern life. And in a dialogue, we get to be aware of that in a collective way.

As long as we have this defensive attitude – blocking and holding assumptions, sticking to them and saying, "I've got to be right," and that sort of thing – then intelligence is very limited, because intelligence requires that you don't defend an assumption. There is no reason to hold to an assumption if there is evidence that it is not right. The proper structure of an assumption or of an opinion is that it is open to evidence that it may not be right.

That does not mean that we are going to impose the opinions of the group. In this way the collective can often be troublesome. The group may act like a conscience, inducing powerful guilt feelings in its members, because we are all so built that we tend to regard what everybody agrees on as true. Everybody may or may not have a different opinion – it is not that important. It isn't necessary that everybody be convinced to have the same view. This sharing of mind, of consciousness, is more important than the content of the opinions. And you may see that these opinions are limited anyway. You may find that the answer is not in the opinions at all, but somewhere else. Truth does not emerge from opinions; it must emerge from something else – perhaps from a more free movement of the tacit mind. So we have to get meanings coherent if we are going to perceive truth, or to take part in truth. That is why I say the dialogue is so important. If our meanings are incoherent, how are we going to participate in truth?

I think this new approach could open the way to changing the whole world situation – ecologically, and in other ways. For instance, the ecological movement, the "green movement," is now in danger of fragmenting and splitting, because many of those groups have different opinions about how to deal with the problems. So they can wind up fighting each other as much as they fight for the ecology. Consequently, it seems particularly urgent that the green movement get into dialogue.

People concerned with the ecology are clearly aware of some of our planetary problems, but I think that many of them may not be as aware of their assumptions and tacit thought processes. I think it is important to call attention to this explicitly in a clear way, so that it becomes clear what the basic problem is. These kinds of activities go together. Cleaning up the rivers and planting trees and saving the whales should go together with dialogue, and with seeing the general problem of thought. They all belong together, because any one of those activities by itself is not enough. If we all just talk about thought and think about thought for a long while, the whole planet may be destroyed in the meantime. But I think that dialogue will work in this tacit level of mental process, where the most significant things take place.

There are situations where people have differing assumptions and opinions, where one faction is interested and the other isn't. Still, somehow, we have got to have a dialogue. Even if one faction won't participate, we who are willing can participate in a dialogue between our thought and their thought. We can at least dialogue among ourselves as far as we can, or you may by yourself. That is the attitude of dialogue. And the further this attitude could spread, the more I think it would help to bring order. If we really could do something creative, it might still affect other people on a tacit level. It would really communicate at the tacit level, both with words and beyond words. But if we keep on repeating the same old story, then it won't happen.

This notion of dialogue and common consciousness suggests that there is some way out of our collective difficulties. And we have to begin at the grass roots, as it were, not to begin at the top of the heap with the United Nations or with the President. I know that there are people in the US State Department who are familiar with this idea of dialogue, which shows how these ideas do percolate and may even reach the highest levels. This indicates that things can communicate very fast in this modern world – though that may look very insignificant at first. In three to five steps it might reach all sorts of levels. Just as the destructive things communicate, so this idea of dialogue could communicate, too.

As we ourselves stay with the frustrations of dialogue, the meaning of what we are doing may be much more than will appear at first sight. In fact, we could say that instead of being part of the problem, we become part of the solution. In other words, our very movement has the quality of the solution; it is part of it. However small it is, it has the quality of the solution and not the quality of the problem. However big the larger movement is, it has the quality of the problem, not of the solution. Accordingly, the major point is to start something which has the quality of the solution. As I have said, we don't know how fast or slowly it would spread. We don't know how fast a movement in the mind – in the thought process and beyond the thought process, this sharing together – will spread.

People sometimes say, "All we really need is love." Of course, that's true – if there were universal love, all would go well. But we don't appear to have it. So we have to find a way that works. Even though there may be frustration and anger and rage and hate and fear, we have to find something which can take all that in.

To illustrate the point, here is a story about the two leading physicists of this century, Albert Einstein and Niels Bohr. Einstein remembered that when he first met Bohr, he felt close to him. He wrote of a feeling of love for him. They talked physics in a very animated way, and so on. But they finally came upon a point where they had two different assumptions, or opinions, about what was the way to truth. Bohr's judgments were based on his view of quantum theory, and Einstein's on his view of relativity. They talked it over again and again in a very patient way, with all goodwill. It went on for years, and neither of them yielded. Each one just repeated what he had been saying before. So finally they found that they weren't getting anywhere, and they gradually drifted apart. They didn't see each other for a long time after that.

Then one year, both of them were at the Institute for Advanced Study at Princeton, but they still didn't meet each other. A mathematician named Herman Weyl said, "It would be nice if they got together. It's a pity that they don't." So he arranged a party to which Einstein and Bohr and their respective students were invited. Einstein and his associates stayed at one end of the room, and Bohr and his associates stayed at the other end. They couldn't get together because they had nothing to talk about. They couldn't share any meaning, because each one felt his meaning was true. How can you share if you are sure you have truth and the other fellow is sure he has truth, and the truths don't agree? How can you share?

Therefore, you have to watch out for the notion of truth. Dialogue may not be concerned directly with truth – it may arrive at truth, but it is concerned with *meaning*. If the meaning is incoherent you will never arrive at truth. You may think, "*My* meaning is coherent and somebody else's isn't," but then we'll never have meaning shared. You will have the "truth" for yourself or for your own group, whatever consolation that is. But we will continue to have conflict.

If it is necessary to share meaning and share truth, then we have to do something different. Bohr and Einstein probably should have had a dialogue. I'm not saying that they *could* have had one, but in a dialogue they might have listened properly to each other's opinion. And perhaps they both would have suspended their opinions, and moved out beyond relativity and beyond quantum theory into something new. They might have done that in principle, but I don't think that this notion of dialogue had occurred to scientists then.

Science is predicated on the concept that science is arriving at truth – at a *unique* truth. The idea of dialogue is thereby in some way foreign to the current structure of science, as it is with religion. In a way, science has become the religion of the modern age. It plays the role which religion used to play of giving us truth; hence different scientists cannot come together any more than different religions can, once they have different notions of truth. As one scientist, Max Planck, said, "New ideas don't win, really. What happens is that the old scientists die and new ones come along with new ideas." But clearly that's not the right way to do it. This is not to say that science couldn't work another way. If scientists could engage in a dialogue, that would be a radical revolution in science – in the very nature of science. Actually, scientists are in principle committed to the concepts involved in dialogue. They say, "We must listen. We shouldn't exclude anything."

However, they find that they can't do that. This is not only because scientists share what everybody else shares – assumptions and opinions – but also because the very notion which has been defining science today is that we are going to *get* truth. Few scientists question the assumption that thought is capable of coming to know "everything." But that may not be a valid assumption, because thought is abstraction, which inherently implies limitation. The *whole* is too much. There is no way by which thought can get hold of the whole, because thought only abstracts; it limits and defines. And the past from which thought draws contains only a certain limited amount. The present is not contained in thought; thus, an analysis cannot actually cover the moment of analysis.

There are also the relativists, who say that we are never going to get at an absolute truth. But they are caught in a paradox of their own. They are assuming that relativism is the absolute truth. So it is clear that people who believe that they are arriving at any kind of absolute truth can't make a dialogue, not even among themselves. Even different relativists don't agree.

So we can see that there is no "road" to truth. What we are trying to say is that in this dialogue we share all the roads and we finally see that none of them matters. We see the meaning of all the roads, and therefore we come to the "no road." Underneath, all the roads are the same because of the very fact that they are "roads" – they are rigid.

We've said that in a dialogue there will be frustrations, but you might become better friends if you can get through all that. Not that we demand affection. We don't demand friendship; we don't demand anything, though friendship may come. *If you see other people's thought, it becomes your own thought, and you treat it as your own thought. And when an emotional charge comes up, you share all the emotional charges, too, if they affect you; you hold them together with all the thoughts.* Often, when there is an emotional charge somebody can come in to defuse the issue a bit so that it doesn't run away – as the child psychiatrist defused it with his asking, "How long will you hate me forever?" Or some other sort of humor may defuse the issue, or something else – some appropriate remark which you can't foresee.

Sometimes you may find that you are about to raise a question, but someone else brings it up. In such a case, that thought is probably latent in the group as a whole, implicit. And one person may say it, or somebody else may say it. Then another person may pick it up and carry it along. If the group is really working, that would be thinking together – common participation in thinking – as if it were all one process. That one thought is being formed together. Then, if somebody comes up with another assumption, we all listen to that, we share that meaning. Now that would be the "vision of dialogue."

SENSITIVITY IN DIALOGUE

What we have been discussing has not been common in human society, although it is really what is necessary if the society is to cohere. If people would do this in government or in business or internationally, our society would work differently. But then, that requires *sensitivity* – a certain way of knowing how to come in and how not to come in, of watching all the subtle cues and the senses and your response to them – what's happening inside of you, what's happening in the group. People may show what is happening to them in the stance of their body – by their "body language" – as well as by what they say.

They are not trying to do this purposefully, but you will find that it develops. That's part of the communication. It will be non-verbal as well as verbal. You're not *trying* to do it at all. You may not even be aware that it is happening.

Sensitivity is being able to sense that something is happening, to sense the way you respond, the way other people respond, to sense the subtle differences and similarities. To sense all this is the foundation of perception. The senses provide you with information, but you have to be sensitive to it or you won't see it. If you know a person very well, you may pass him on the street and say, "I saw him." If you are asked what the person was wearing, however, you may not know, because you didn't really look. You were not sensitive to all that, because you saw that person through the *screen of thought*. And that was not sensitivity.

So sensitivity involves the senses, and also something beyond. The senses are sensitive to certain things to which they respond, but that's not enough. The senses will tell you what is happening, and then the consciousness must build a form, or create some sense of what it *means*, which holds it together. Therefore, meaning is part of it. You are sensitive to the meaning, or to the lack of meaning. It's perception of meaning, if you want to put it that way. In other words, it is a more subtle perception. The meaning is what holds it together. As I said, it is the "cement." Meaning is not static – it is flowing. And if we have the meaning being shared, then it is flowing among us; it holds the group together. Then everybody is sensitive to all the nuances going around, not merely to what is happening in his own mind. From that forms a meaning which is shared. And in that way we can talk together coherently and think together. Whereas generally people hold to their assumptions, so they are not thinking together. Each one is on his own.

What blocks sensitivity is the defense of your assumptions and opinions. But if you are defending your opinions, you don't judge yourself and say, "I shouldn't be defending." Rather, the fact is that you *are* defending, and you then need to be sensitive to that – to all the feelings in that, all the subtle nuances. We are not aiming for the type of group that condemns and judges, and so forth – we can all realize that that would get in the way. So this group is not going to judge or condemn. It is simply going to look at all the opinions and assumptions and let them surface. And I think that there could then be a change.

Krishnamurti said that "to be" is to be related. But relationship can be very painful. He said that you have to think/feel out all your mental processes and work them through, and then that will open the way to something else. And I think that is what can happen in the dialogue group. Certain painful things can happen for some people; you have to work it all out.

We once had a dialogue in Sweden, in which the group seemed to divide itself into two factions. There were a lot of

"New Age" people, and from the beginning they began to talk about the virtues of love and the fact that the place was full of love all around, that it was all love everywhere. Part of the group remained silent for a while, but in the next hour they started to talk. They intimated that the love talk was all sentimental nonsense and didn't mean anything. Then one fellow got so excited that he couldn't stand it, and he walked out. He eventually came back, and they finally got together again. Polarization had taken place, which is a typical difficulty that can arise. Someone noticed the polarization happening and said with a bit of good humor, "There are two groups here – the love group and the hate group." That broke the tension a little, and the two sides could then begin to talk. They didn't necessarily convince each other, but each was able to see the meaning of the other side's position, and the two polarized groups were able to talk to each other.

Now, *that* was a more important point than whether they convinced each other. They might find that they both have to give up their positions so that something else can come about. It was not important whether one favored love or one favored hate or another favored being suspicious and careful and somewhat cynical, or whatever. Really, underneath they were similar, because they both had rigid positions. Loosening that position, then, was the key change.

On the whole, you could say that if you are defending your opinions, you are not serious. Likewise, if you are trying to avoid something unpleasant inside of yourself, that is also not being serious. A great deal of our whole life is not serious. And society teaches you that. It teaches you *not* to be very serious – that there are all sorts of incoherent things, and there is nothing that can be done about it, and that you will only stir yourself up uselessly by being serious.

But in a dialogue you have to be serious. It is not a dialogue if you are not – not in the way I'm using the word. There is a story about Freud when he had cancer of the mouth. Somebody came up to him and wanted to talk to him about a point in psychology. The person said, "Perhaps I'd better not talk to you, because you've got this cancer which is very serious. You may not want to talk about this." Freud's answer was, "This cancer may be fatal, but it's not serious." And actually, of course, it was just a lot of cells growing. I think a great deal of what goes on in society could be described that way – that it may well be fatal, but it's not serious.

LIMITED DIALOGUE

Sometimes people feel a sense of dialogue within their families. But a family is generally a hierarchy, organized on the principle of authority which is contrary to dialogue. The family is a very authoritative structure, based on obligation, and that sort of thing. It has its value, but it is a structure within which it might be difficult to get dialogue going. It would be good if you could – perhaps that could happen in some families. In general it is difficult, though, because there is no place in the dialogue for the principle of authority and hierarchy. We want to be free of hierarchy and authority as we move. You must have *some* authority to "run" things; that's why we say that if you have a "purpose," then you are bound to bring in some authority somewhere. But in dialogue, insofar as we have no purpose and no agenda and we don't have to *do* anything, we don't really need to have an authority or a hierarchy. Rather, we need a place where there is no authority, no hierarchy, where there is no special purpose – sort of an empty place, where we can let anything be talked about.

As we said, you can also have a dialogue in a more limited way – perhaps with a purpose or a goal in mind. It would be best to accept the principle of letting it be open, because when you limit it, you are accepting assumptions on the basis of which you limit it – assumptions that may actually be getting in the way of free communication. So you are not looking at those assumptions.

However, if people are not ready to be completely open in their communication, they should do what they can. I know some university professors who are interested in applying the principles of dialogue to corporate problems. One of them recently had a meeting with the executive officers of a corporation that makes office furniture. They wanted to have this sort of meeting, because they knew that they were not functioning efficiently and that they couldn't agree. The higher officers had all sorts of assumptions that blocked everything. So they asked him to come in. He started a dialogue which they found very interesting, and now they want to have a whole series of them.

Naturally, that sort of dialogue will be limited – the people involved do have a definite purpose, which is limiting – but even so, it has considerable value. The principle is at least to get people to come to know each other's assumptions, so they can listen to their assumptions and know what they are. Very often people get into problems where they don't really know what the other person's assumption is, and they react according to what they think it is. That person then gets very puzzled and wonders: what is he doing? He reacts, and it all gets very muddled. So it is valuable if they can at least get to realize each other's assumptions.

The professor told me about two interesting cases. One involved a company which had trouble with people in the higher executive branches who were not very happy and were not getting on with each other. The company's usual way of solving it was to offer them a higher salary, sort of a sweetener, and a lot of mediocre people were given the very highest possible positions. It went on and on, and pretty soon there were so many people with high salaries that the company couldn't afford it; they were failing. They said, "What can we do? Well, we've got to have somebody who's tough, who will tell these people, 'You have to accept another position.' " The negotiator that they used explained the new policies by saying, "The company just can't afford it." But he was avoiding the issue. He was not straightforwardly saying, "This whole approach is wrong." Now, if the company is to work efficiently, there must be a mutual agreement that they are not going to give a person a higher position just to alleviate a psychological problem between people. That's not a right way to proceed. Everybody should understand that that is not the right way of working, otherwise the company won't succeed. Therefore, a dialogue was needed so that they could really begin talking with each other in order to come to see clearly the salient points: "That's the way we are thinking, that's where the problems are coming from, and that's the way we have to go." So within the framework of assuming that the company has to survive, there was a limited kind of dialogue – not the kind we ultimately want to have here, but still it was good in some way.

Now, I am suggesting that the human race has got to do that.

We could say that the human race is failing for the same sort of reason that the company was failing.

The second case involved the negotiating group itself, the university people whose specialty it is to go into companies and help solve these problems. They were organizing a meeting among themselves with the same purpose – just so they could talk. They had a series of meetings where it happened that two of their people could never quite meet on any issue. One of them constantly had the assumption that the right thing to do was to bring out the trouble – to confront somebody with it. And the other person had the opposite assumption, which was that you shouldn't do that. He wanted other people to draw him out. He felt that he couldn't say something unless other people created the space for him to talk, and drew him out. The first fellow wouldn't do that, he did the opposite. So they couldn't meet. The whole thing went on for a long time in confusion, with the one person waiting to be drawn out, and the other person not understanding that this was the case. Finally they got to talking, and each one actually brought up childhood experiences which were behind his assumptions – and then it opened up.

The fellow who was working as facilitator during this time did very little. In fact, several of the people appealed to the facilitator and said, "Why don't you talk?" The facilitator may come in from time to time and comment on what is going on or what it all means. In a more general group he should eventually be able to be just a participant. Probably in the company group this wouldn't work, though; he couldn't become *just* a participant – such a group has too limited an objective.

This second example might be an illustration of when the personal may have to come into the general, because in certain cases there are blocks due to particular assumptions that the person got hold of in childhood, or in some other way. And in this example, they were finally able to uncover those assumptions. They weren't trying to heal each other, or to do therapy; nevertheless, it had a therapeutic effect. But that's a secondary thing.

Some people feel that that type of corporate dialogue is only furthering a corrupt system. However, there is a germ of something different. I think that if you go into society, you will find that almost everything is involved in this corrupt game. So it doesn't accomplish anything to dismiss it all. The executives have got to make the company work; and in fact, if all these companies would work more efficiently we would all be a lot better off. It's partly because they are in such a mess that we are in trouble, that society is inefficient, that the whole thing is falling apart. If the government and the companies could all work efficiently, we wouldn't be so wasteful, even though that by itself wouldn't solve all the problems.

For the society to be working right, all those things have got to work efficiently and coherently. If we look at what is going on in the world today, in this or in any country, we can say that it is not working coherently. Most companies are not really working coherently. And slowly the thing is sinking. I think that if you can get this notion across in whatever situation – the germ of the notion of dialogue – if you can get people to look at it, it's a step. You could say that heads of state are not likely to have the kind of dialogue that we are talking about. But if they will have any kind at all, if they'll begin to accept this principle, it's a step. It may make a change; for instance, the kind of waste of energy which is going on in the production of armaments could be cut down. If we could stop the tremendous amount that's being spent on armaments – let's say a trillion dollars a year – that could be used for ecological regeneration and all sorts of constructive things. And possibly some of that might happen. Those political figures who are more aware of the ecological problem might, for instance, make the President more aware of it, if they would really talk. Not that we can expect the politicians to solve the problems we face. But I'm saying that if there's a slight movement toward something more open, the rate of destruction will slow down. If we go on at this rate, we may have very little time to do anything.

We can't do anything at the level of presidents or prime ministers. They have their own opinions. But the various ideas filter, as we've said. Somehow the notion of something a little bit like dialogue has filtered to that level, and it may have an effect; that's all I am saying. I think that in the US government there are some people who are more this way, and some people who are more the other way. We don't know how it is going to come out, but there is a certain movement toward something more open. I don't say that it is going to solve the whole thing; I am saying that if it slows down the destruction, that's important, because unless the destruction is slowed down to give time for something new to emerge, it will be too late.

There may be no pat political answer to the world's problems. However, the important point is not the answer – just as in a dialogue, the important point is not the particular opinions – but rather the softening up, the opening up of the mind, and looking at all the opinions. If there is some sort of spread of that attitude, I think it can slow down the destruction.

So we've said that it is crucial to be able to share our judgments, to share our assumptions, to listen to each other's assumptions. In the case of Einstein and Bohr it didn't lead to violence that they did not; but in general, if somebody doesn't listen to your basic assumptions you feel it as an act of violence, and then you are inclined to be violent yourself. Therefore, this is crucial both individually and collectively. Dialogue is the collective way of opening up judgments and assumptions.

BEYOND DIALOGUE

We should keep in mind, nonetheless, that the dialogue – and in fact, all that we've been talking about – is not only directed at solving the ills of society, although we do have to solve those ills. We would be much better off if we didn't have them. If we survive and we want to have a worthwhile life, we have to deal with those problems. But ultimately that's not the entire story. That's only the beginning. I'm suggesting that there is the possibility for a transformation of the nature of consciousness, both individually and collectively, and that whether this can be solved culturally and socially depends on dialogue. That's what we're exploring.

And it's very important that it happens together, because if one individual changes it will have very little general effect. But if it happens collectively, it means a lot more. If some of us come to the "truth," so-called, while a lot of people are left out, it's not going to solve the problem. We would have another conflict – just as there is conflict between different parts of the Christian faith or the Muhammadan faith or various others, even though they all believe in the same God, the same prophet or the same savior.

Love will go away if we can't communicate and share meaning. The love between Einstein and Bohr gradually evaporated because they could not communicate. However, if we can really communicate, then we will have fellowship, participation, friendship, and love, growing and growing. That would be the way. The question is really: do you see the necessity of this process? That's the key question. If you see that it is absolutely necessary, then you have to do something.

And perhaps in dialogue, when we have this very high energy of coherence, it might bring us beyond just being a group that could solve social problems. Possibly it could make a new change in the individual and a change in the relation to the cosmic. Such an energy has been called "communion." It is a kind of participation. The early Christians had a Greek word, *koinonia*, the root of which means "to participate" – the idea of partaking of the whole and taking part in it; not merely the whole group, but the *whole*.

3

THE NATURE OF
COLLECTIVE THOUGHT

What are the troubles of the world? They seem so many that
we can hardly begin even to list them. We can see wars going
on, starvation, torture, pillage, disease, all sorts of dirty tricks
played in politics. We have a kind of polarization between East
and West – the West professes the value of the individual and
freedom, and the East professes the value of the collective
society, with everybody being taken care of. We have the North/
South polarization – the North is more wealthy and the South
less so. There's tremendous trouble in Africa and South America
and southern parts of Asia; there's very great poverty and
indebtedness and a breakdown of the economy and general
chaos in what's going on there.

With advancing technology you have the possibility that
nuclear bombs will perhaps be available to all sorts of dictators,
even in relatively small nations. There are biological and chemical weapons, and other kinds of weapons that have not yet been
invented, but surely will. And we have the danger of ecological
destruction – destruction of agricultural land and forests, pollution, the change of climate, and many other things. There
could be a real ecological disaster within not too long a period
of time if people keep doing whatever they're doing. Then we
have the growth of crime and violence everywhere – drugs and
so on – indicating that people are very unhappy and not satisfied. I don't need to multiply it. The list could be extended
almost indefinitely.

Why have we accepted this state of affairs which is so destructive and so dangerous and so conducive to unhappiness? It
seems we're mesmerized in some way. We go on with this
insanity and nobody seems to know what to do or say. In the

past people used to hope that some solution would appear, such as democracy or socialism or something else, perhaps religion; but this hopeful state of mind is very much weakened now because it has not worked out at all. I am suggesting that underneath it there's something we don't understand about how thought works.

In the beginning of the process of civilization, thought was regarded as a very valuable thing. And it still is. Thought has done all the things which we are proud of. It has built our cities (we shouldn't be so proud of them, I suppose). It has created science and technology, and has been very creative in medicine. Practically all of what has been called nature has been arranged by thought. Yet thought also goes wrong somehow, and produces destruction. This arises from a certain way of thinking, i.e., *fragmentation*. This is to break things up into bits, as if they were independent. It's not merely making divisions, but it is breaking things up which are not really separate. It's like taking a watch and smashing it into fragments, rather than taking it apart and finding its parts. The parts are parts of a *whole*, but the fragments are just arbitrarily broken off from each other. Things which really fit, and belong together, are treated as if they do not. That's one of the features of thought that's going wrong.

In the past, people may not have noticed this, and may have thought only that "knowledge is power" and ignorance is bad. But there's a certain danger in knowledge and in thought, which people haven't paid enough attention to. Thought may have started to go wrong thousands or tens of thousands of years ago – we don't know. But now technology has gone so far that it has really become deadly. If you imagine a thousand years of what's going on now, what will happen? Will there not be some catastrophe or another? Therefore, with the growth of technology the human race is faced with a tremendous crisis, or challenge. We have got to do something about this thought process – we can't just let it go on destroying us. But then, what do you do about it? You can't cut out thought – clearly we couldn't do without it. And you can't just select all the bad thoughts and cut them out. So we have to go into it more deeply. I say this is not an obvious thing – it's very subtle and it goes very deep. We want to get to the root of it, to the base, to the source of it.

Imagine a stream which is being polluted near the source. The people downstream don't know about that, so they start removing bits of pollution, trying to purify their water, but perhaps introducing more pollution of another kind as they do so. What has to be done, therefore, is to see this whole stream, and get to the source of it. Somewhere, at the source of thought, it is being polluted – that is the suggestion. Pollution is being diverted into the stream, and this is happening all the time. You could say, in one sense, the wrong step was when people first started pouring pollution in. But the fact that we have kept on pouring it in is the main point – it's pouring in all the time. Therefore, the source is not in time – not back in ancient times, when it may have started – but rather the source is always *now*. That's what we have to look into.

I would say further that we want to *see* something about thought: we not only want to talk about thought and think about thought, but we want to see something about how thought actually works – beyond the word. You may not know what I mean by that. I mean that thought is a real process, and that we have got to be able to pay attention to it as we pay attention to processes taking place outside in the material world, in the world that we can see. We may not know what that means, to pay attention to thought. Neither our culture, nor indeed hardly any culture, is able to give much help on that, and yet that is crucial. Everything depends on thought – if thought goes wrong, we're going to do everything wrong. But we are so used to taking it for granted that we don't pay any attention to it.

If you say, "This is too big for me," in one sense that's true. In another sense, I say it's not. If you say the crisis is only the external phenomenon – what's going on in the outside world – then it's very big. It's like this: suppose you have a dam which has not been constructed properly, and it slowly erodes away. Then it suddenly goes, and that wall of water is running down. Indeed, you're not going to be able to stop it at that moment. But the question is – what about the process which is constantly making the wrong kind of dam and letting it erode? What's going on deeper down?

The real crisis is not in these events which are confronting us, like wars and crime and drugs and economic chaos and pollution; it's really in the thought which is making it – all the time. Each person can do something about that thought, because he's in it. But one of the troubles we get into is to say, "It's they who are thinking all that, and I am thinking right." I say that's a mistake. I say thought *pervades* us. It's similar to a virus – somehow this is a disease of thought, of knowledge, of information, spreading all over the world. The more computers, radio, and television we have, the faster it spreads. So the kind of thought that's going on all around us begins to take over in every one of us, without our even noticing it. It's spreading like a virus and each one of us is nourishing that virus.

Do we have a kind of immune system that stops it? The only way to stop it is to recognize it, to acknowledge it, to see what it is. If any one of us starts to look at that, then we are looking at the source of the problem. It's the same in all of us. We may imagine that the source of the problem is that somebody "over there" is thinking these wrong thoughts – or that a lot of people are. But the source of the problem is much deeper. It is that something is going wrong in the whole process of thought, which is collective, which belongs to all of us.

A key assumption that we have to question is that our thought is our own individual thought. Now, to some extent it is. We have some independence. But we must look at it more carefully. It's more subtle than to say it's individual or it's not individual. We have to see what thought *really* is, without presuppositions. What is really going on when we're thinking? I'm trying to say that most of our thought in its general form is not individual. It originates in the whole culture and it pervades us. We pick it up as children from parents, from friends, from school, from newspapers, from books, and so on. We make a small change in it; we select certain parts of it which we like, and we may reject other parts. But still, it all comes from that pool. This deep structure of thought, which is the source, the constant source – timeless – is always there. It's not that we go back in time to find its origin, but rather that it's constantly working. This deep structure of thought is what is common, and this is what we have to get at. We will have to come to see that the content of thought and the deep structure are not really separate, because the way we think about thought has an effect on its structure. If we think, for example, that thought is coming from *me* individually, this will affect how thought works. So we have to look at both content and structure.

51

We have the sense that we "know" all sorts of things. But we could say that perhaps it is not "we," but *knowledge itself* which knows all sorts of things. The suggestion is that knowledge – which is thought – is moving autonomously: it passes from one person to another. There is a whole pool of knowledge for the whole human race, like different computers that share a pool of knowledge. This pool of thought has been developing for many thousands of years, and it is full of all sorts of content. This knowledge, or thought, knows all of that content, *but it doesn't know what it is doing.* This knowledge knows itself wrongly: it knows itself as doing nothing. It therefore says, "I am not responsible for any of these problems. I'm just here for you to use."

All of this thought, which is based on what one has been thinking, is clearly coming from memory. You build up knowledge through experience, through practice. You think about it, you organize it, it goes into memory and becomes knowledge. Part of that knowledge is skill, through practice – that too is a kind of memory, somewhere in the body or in the brain. It's all part of one system. In this connection, there is what Michael Polanyi has called *tacit knowledge* – the knowledge which you can't state in words, but which is there. You know how to ride a bicycle, but you can't state how. If a bicycle is falling, you have to turn it in the direction it's falling in order to make it come up. Mathematically, there is a formula that shows that the angle to which you turn is related in a certain way to the angle at which you're falling. This is what you'll actually do, *but you don't work out the formula.* Your whole body does countless movements that you can't describe, and it makes it all work. That's tacit knowledge. It's a kind of knowledge you've got, without which you could do nothing. It's a continuation from the past of something that you learned. So we have experience, knowledge, thought, emotion, practice – all one process.

Further, in our language we have a distinction between "thinking" and "thought." 'Thinking" implies the present tense – some activity going on which may include critical sensitivity to what can go wrong. Also there may be new ideas, and perhaps occasionally perception of some kind inside. "Thought" is the past participle of that. We have the idea that after we have been thinking something, it just evaporates. But thinking doesn't disappear. It goes somehow into the brain and leaves something – a trace – which becomes thought. And thought then acts automatically. So thought is the response from memory – from the past, from what has been done. Thus we have thinking and thought.

We also have the word "feeling." Its present tense suggests the active present, that the feeling is directly in contact with reality. But it might be useful to introduce the word "felt," to say there are "feelings" and "felts." That is, "felts" are feelings which have been recorded. A traumatic experience in the past can make you feel very uncomfortable when remembered. Nostalgic feelings are also from the past. A lot of the feelings that come up are really from the past, they're "felts." But if they are just a recording being replayed, they don't have as much significance as if they were a response to the present immediate situation.

It's really very important to see that our culture gives us a wrong lead about thoughts and felts. It constantly tends to imply that they could be separated and that one could control the other. But thoughts and felts are one process; they are not two. They both come from the memory; in the memory they are probably all mixed. Memory also affects the physical body. It affects the sensations. You can produce states of stress in the body from memory of states of stress. Therefore, when memory acts you cannot separate the intellectual function, the emotional function, the chemical function, the muscular function – because this *tacit knowledge* is also a kind of memory – they're all there.

Neuroscientific studies of brain structure suggest that thought originates somewhere in the outer cortex of the brain – in the prefrontal lobes – and that the emotional center is deeper down. There is a very thick bundle of nerves connecting them, and in this way they should be closely related; there is a lot of evidence that they are. Consider the primitive reflex to fight or to run or to freeze. There was a nice example of how this works under modern conditions in a television program which, among other things, showed an airport controller who is angry at his boss. His boss is mistreating him. He can't run, because he has to stay there. He can't fight his boss. And he can't just stop and freeze and do nothing. Meanwhile, the brain is pouring neurochemicals into the system, *as if he were being attacked in the jungle.* This process is stirring up the body and making it all work rather badly, and also preventing rational thought because such thought requires a nice, quiet brain. The more he thinks, the worse it gets. He'll get thoughts which lead him further astray and make more trouble.

It would be interesting to trace the evolution and show the steps that brought this all about. As a theory, you could say that our "new brain," with the forebrain and the cortex which allows for complex thought, developed rather rapidly; and therefore it did not come into a harmonious relationship with what was there before. The older functions of the brain, such as emotions and so on, could respond to the immediate fact of the animal's environment: run, fight, or freeze. Then came the activity of this new cortex, which could project images of all kinds which were very realistic; but the "old brain" had never learned very well how to tell the difference between an image and reality, *because it had no need to*. It had never been surrounded by a structure that would produce a lot of images. It was like a dog that would never have to imagine another dog when it wasn't looking at it.

When we evolved to the chimpanzee – which could think of other chimpanzees even when they were not there – then the *image* of the other chimpanzee could produce the same reaction as the chimpanzee itself. This began to confuse the new part of the brain, due to "fight, run, freeze," reactions, neurochemicals, and so on. The new brain couldn't get things straight, and it further tangled up the old brain. It all began to build up a series of entrained mistakes, one after another.

So perhaps this is one of the ways we got to where we are. The thing to notice is that the major environment of the old brain is now, not nature, but *the new brain*, because nature is now filtered through the new brain. Civilization tends to make this worse – that's clear. As civilization develops, you have to have a bigger society with rules, authority, police, jails, armies. You build up a tremendous amount of stress. And the further civilization goes, by and large, the greater the stress. It has been that way for millennia, and we haven't solved the problem of what to do about it.

You could ask, "Why don't people see this clearly? It seems a very present danger and yet it seems people can't see it." They don't see it because of this thought process, which is collective as well as individual. The thoughts, the fantasies, and the collective fantasies are entering perception. Myths are collective fantasies, and every culture has its myths. Many of them are entering perception as if they were perceived realities. Everybody has a somewhat different way in which this happens, and we don't actually see the fact. *That* is the fact: that we don't see the fact. There is a higher order of fact – which is that we are not seeing the direct fact. This is the fact from which we must start.

I think we can get a further insight into why concepts and images have such a powerful effect, if we more fully consider that thought is able to provide a *representation* of what we experience. "Representation" is a very appropriate word here, because it just says "re-present" – to present again. Thus, we may say that perception *presents* something, and that thought *re-presents* it in abstraction.

A map is a kind of representation. The map is obviously much less than the territory it represents. This abstraction is advantageous because it focuses on what may be important for our purposes, with all the unnecessary detail left out. It is structured and organized in a way which may be helpful and relevant. Therefore, a representation is not just *a* concept – it's really a number of concepts together.

Another example would be the case of someone giving a talk – there forms in the minds of those who listen a representation of whatever is meant. In listening to someone who is describing something, some sort of representation will form in your mind – in the imagination perhaps – as if it were perceived. It will not be the same as the thing itself – it will be very abstract compared with it. It will highlight certain points, which may be of interest compared to the original perception, and so on. We are constantly forming re-presentations in this way.

But the thing to notice – the key point – is that this representation is not only present in thought or in imagination, but *it fuses with the actual perception or experience.* In other words, the representation fuses with the "presentation," so that what is "presented" (as perception) is already in large part a re-presentation. So it "presents again." You then get what we might call a "net presentation," which is the result of the senses, of thought, and possibly some insight. It all comes together in one net presentation. The way you experience something, therefore, depends on how you represent it – or mis-represent it.

If you represent yourself to yourself as noble and capable and honest, that representation enters the perception of yourself. That's how you perceive yourself. Now, somebody else gives another representation – which is that you are dishonest and stupid – and this goes in, too, and affects your "perception" of yourself. And that shakes up the whole neurophysiological system in a very disturbing way. Thought is then under pressure to represent the situation in a better light – and there you see the beginning of self-deception.

We generally do not notice the connection between representation and presentation – the two-way connection. Thought seems to lack the ability to see that this is happening. The process is unconscious, implicit, tacit – we don't know exactly how it happens. But we can see that something happens in which thought mixes these up. Imagine the information coming in from the senses and being organized in the brain, but then another stream of information comes in from thought, and the two mix in the whole. The net presentation is a result of the two.

The important point is that we are not aware that this is happening. The human race by and large has seldom known this – if ever. Perhaps a few people have known it, but by and large we go ahead without being aware of it. We're not saying that this process is bad or good. What's wrong with it is not that it takes place, but rather that we are not aware of it.

Now, we couldn't do without the connection between representation and presentation. In order to take action toward something, it's not enough to represent it only in imagination or thought. You must actually feel it to be present in your perception. Take the example of a forest. It could be represented as a source of lumber, and it would then be presented to a lumberman in that way. To the artist it could be represented as something worth painting. To someone who wants to take a walk, it would be represented as a place he could enjoy himself walking along the path. There are countless representations of the forest, which will *present* the forest in different ways.

What is not represented as interesting generally does not hold your interest. If it is not represented as valuable and interesting, it is not presented in that way, and therefore it doesn't hold the interest. And in some cases you *should* represent it according to your interest. You may say, "I need to represent it in a certain way to do something." It will therefore hold your interest and attention while you're doing it. Now, none of this is wrong. In fact, all of it is absolutely necessary. Unless something is presented in that way, you can't take action. You can't just act from the abstract representation in the imagination. You have got to act from the concrete presentation.

But the lack of awareness of this process is crucial. If someone says, "People of this category are bad," and you accept that, then *the representation of thought enters the presentation of perception.* Once you've accepted that, it goes into implicit, tacit thought. The next moment, when you see a person of that kind, it comes up as a presentation. The "badness" is perceived as inhering in him. It is not that you say, "I know that somebody has *told* me that these people are bad, and they may be bad or they may be good. I'd better look and see." But rather, what they "are" is apparently right "there." From there on, you think about that as if it were entirely an independent fact – independent of thought.

Thought then begins apparently to *prove* itself, and to create "facts" which are not really facts. The Latin root of the word "fact" means "what has been made," as in "manufacture." In some sense we have to establish a fact, but this sort of fact is being made wrongly. This is a fact which is, so to speak, not being properly manufactured. It's being made in the wrong way because we are mixing up thought into that "fact," and not knowing that we are doing it. It's necessary to let thought enter the fact, but we fail to notice that this is happening. If we say it's a "pure" fact, which is just "there," we will give it tremendous value, and say, "How can you deny the fact? You can see what sort of people they are."

It is important to see that most of our representations arise collectively, and that gives them greater power. If everybody agrees on something, we take that as evidence that it's right, or that it could be right. This then creates a pressure on us – we don't want to get out of the consensus. This means that we are constantly under pressure to accept any particular representation, and to see it that way. For example, what we call the "self" is represented in a certain way, and therefore presented in a certain way. This representation is basically collective, in the sense that the general properties of the self are determined collectively, and particular details are determined individually. The consensus all over the world is that you have a self, because all the evidence is that you've got one. It's on your birth certificate – you've got a name, you're identified. In many countries you have an identity card. You've got a bank account, you've got land, you've got a profession, and so on. All of this is representing what you *are*, and therefore it is presenting what you are.

Another example would be a rainbow – everybody sees the same rainbow. There's a collective representation of the rainbow – we all have a consensus about it. But physics, which looks at things "literally," says, "No, there is no rainbow. There are a lot of droplets of water, the sun is in back of you and it's being reflected and refracted off the water and forming colors. In seeing this, each person is forming his own perception of a rainbow. It happens they all look very similar, therefore they all think they're all looking at the same rainbow." (You could also argue that by adopting that view you are taking *physics* as the real thing.) The point, though, is that a lot of our collective representations – a country, a religion, General Motors, the ego – are of the same quality as the rainbow. A great many things which we take as solid reality are very similar to the rainbow. In fact, it's not wrong to do that. The difficulty arises because we do not realize that this is happening, and we therefore give the representation the value of independent fact. If we could see it happening, it would produce no problem at all. We would then be able to value the "fact" for whatever it is. But in our current approach, we are able to take "facts" which have very little value, and value them very highly.

We've applied this notion to a few simple cases, many of which are outside of us. But going further, getting more of a feeling for this notion, you begin to see how it works inside of us and between us – in communication and in dialogue. You see that this question of representation is crucial in our communication. Suppose people meet in a group, bringing certain representations about what other people are like, or what they themselves are like. As the group communicates, these representations may get shaken, and change; the presentation changes, and therefore the whole relationship changes. Our relationship depends on how we present other people to ourselves, and how we present ourselves to other people. And all of that depends on the general collective representations.

When things are going smoothly there is no way to know that there's anything wrong – we have already made the assumption that what's going on is independent of thought. When things are represented, and then presented in that way, there is no way for you to see what is happening – it's already excluded. You cannot pay attention to what is outside the representation. There's tremendous pressure not to; it's very hard. The only time you can pay attention to it is when you see there is trouble – when a surprise comes, when there's a contradiction, when things don't quite work.

However, we don't want to view this process as a "problem," because we have no idea how to *solve* it – we can't project a solution. One of our representations is that everything we do is in time. We project a goal and we find the means to achieve the end. Therefore everything in the world is presented that way – as something that could be handled in that way. We should, then, think of this as a question, or a difficulty – seeing that things are not working right. We're beginning to see where it's going wrong, though perhaps not yet being able to really change it. But we're starting to get some sort of feeling for where it's going wrong – namely, that a lot of what we take to be fact is not really fact.

This implies a different way of seeing the world – it implies that our whole way of seeing the world could change. We see the world according to the general collective representations circulating around our society and culture, and insofar as these could be dropped, then we may change, because the world is presented differently. If you are presented to me as a dangerous person, then I will shrink back – I can't help it. But if I represent you differently, then my whole approach is different. Further, we have to be careful about mis-representation. We could say, "We are all loving one another, everything is solved." That would then be presented, and we would get a nice glow; however, this would be based on a *mis*-representation. But this doesn't change the fact that any real change in presentation – any *genuine* change – is a change of being.

We could consider a representation which is current in our society, such as, "You have to take care of yourself first, you have to watch out – people are dangerous – you can't trust them," and so on. This will produce a response, not only outwardly but also inwardly. The entire neurochemistry develops accordingly, as does the tension in the body. Now, it's true that the world is dangerous, but we are looking at this wrongly. It's dangerous not because people are intrinsically dangerous, but because of mis-representation that has generally been accepted. We have to see the right reason. Therefore, we don't approach such people as intrinsically dangerous, but as people who are the victims of mis-representation.

Changing this representation then opens the way to further change. We don't say it's going to be easy, or hard – we don't know – but it opens up the way, it opens up a big perspective. If we could learn to see thought actually producing presentations from representations, we would no longer be fooled by it – it would be like seeing the trick of a magician. As long as you don't see what the magician is doing, it seems like magic. But if you had a direct insight into the trick, it could change everything.

Many worlds are possible – it all depends on representation, especially the collective representation. To make a "world" takes more than one person, and therefore the collective representation is the key. It's not enough merely for one person to change his representation. That's fine, but we're saying that the real change is the change of collective representations.

4

THE PROBLEM AND THE PARADOX

We have been looking at the vast range of problems facing humanity. These go on proliferating indefinitely, eventually leading on toward disorders of world-wide scope. On contemplating this general situation, one may even sometimes have a sense of being confronted by difficulties beyond the possibility of resolution by human intelligence and co-operative endeavor.

In this mass of contradiction and confusion, one finds a very curious common denominator: i.e., that everyone appears to agree that what is actually confronting us is a set of *problems*. Generally speaking, one does not find that people have considered the question of whether the word "problem," with all that it signifies, provides an adequate description of what is going wrong in human affairs. Yet, if one goes into the meaning of the word, one can see good reason to raise such a question, and to suspect that the attempt to treat our current difficulties as "problems" may be one of the more important factors preventing these difficulties from being properly brought to an end.

The root of "problem" is a Greek word whose meaning is "to put forward." Indeed, this is the essential significance of the word: i.e., to put forward for discussion or questioning an idea that is suggested toward the resolution of certain difficulties or inadequacies. Thus, if one needs to reach a certain destination, one may suggest taking a train, and one can discuss the problem of meeting the train on time, paying for the ticket, etc. Similarly, sailing ships were seen to be a slow and unreliable means of transport, and so men put forth the idea of driving ships by steam, thus giving rise to the problem of how to realize this idea technically and how to carry it out practically. More generally, it is clear that a large part of our practical and technical activities

61

are centered on work aimed at solving a wide range of such problems.

However, when one puts forth an idea in the form of a problem, there are certain largely tacit and implicit presuppositions which must be satisfied if the activity is to make sense. Among these is of course the assumption that the questions raised are rational and free of contradiction. Sometimes, without our noticing it, we accept absurd problems with false or self-contradictory presuppositions. In the practical and technical realm, however, we can usually sooner or later detect that our question is absurd, and we then drop the "problem" as meaningless. Thus, for a long time, people sought to invent a machine capable of perpetual motion, but with the development of scientific understanding it became clear that this would be in contradiction with the basic laws of physics, and so the search for such a machine has ceased.

All of this is fairly clear in the practical and technical domain. But now, what is to be done when one goes on to consider psychological problems and problems of human relationship? Does it make sense to formulate problems of such a kind? Or is this domain not one in which the presuppositions behind the questions put forth for discussion are false, self-contradictory, and absurd?

Consider, for example, a man who suddenly realized that he was very susceptible to flattery. He might well put forth the idea that he ought to be immune to flattery, and then he would of course have the problem of overcoming his tendency to "fall" for anyone who told him how wonderful a person he was. It takes only a little consideration, however, to see that this "problem" is based on absurd presuppositions. For example, the origin of the wish to be flattered is often a deep sense of being inadequate, which is so painful that awareness of its very existence is largely suppressed, except for certain moments in which criticisms or some other indications of a similar nature momentarily call attention to this very unpleasant feeling. As soon as someone comes along and tells such a person that, after all, he is good, capable, wise, beautiful, etc., then the deadening sense of suppressed pain disappears, to be replaced by a buoyant feeling of pleasure and well-being. Along with this goes a tendency to believe that he is being told the truth: for otherwise, of course, there would be no such release. In order to "defend" himself from the "danger" of discovering that it is not the truth, such a person is then ready to believe all that he is told by the other person, and thus, as is well known, he opens himself to the possibility of being taken advantage of in countless ways.

In essence, what goes wrong in flattery is a subtle kind of self-deception. If such a person were then to put forth "the problem" of how he can stop deceiving himself, the absurdity of this procedure would become self-evident. For it is clear that even if he tries hard and makes an effort to overcome his tendency to self-deception, this very effort will be infected with the wish for a pleasurable release from pain that is at the origin of the whole tendency in the first place. So he will almost certainly deceive himself about the question of whether he has overcome self-deception or not.

More generally, one can say that when something goes wrong psychologically, it is confusing to describe the resulting situation as a "problem." Rather, it would be better to say that one was confronted by a *paradox*. In the case of the man who is susceptible to flattery, the paradox is that he apparently knows and understands the absolute need to be honest with himself and yet he feels an even stronger "need" to deceive himself, when this helps to release him from an unbearable sense of inadequacy and to substitute instead a sense of inward rightness and well-being. What is called for in such a case is not some procedure that "solves his problem." Rather, it is to pause and to give attention to the fact that his thinking and feeling is dominated, through and through, by a set of self-contradictory demands or "needs" so that as long as such thinking and feeling prevail, there is *no* way to put things right. It takes a great deal of energy and seriousness to "stay with" an awareness of this fact, rather than to "escape" by allowing the mind to dart into some other subject, or otherwise lose awareness of the actual state of affairs. Such attention, going immensely beyond what is merely verbal or intellectual, can actually bring the root of the paradox into awareness, and thus the paradox dissolves when its nullity and absurdity are clearly seen, felt, and understood.

It has to be emphasized, however, that as long as a paradox is treated as a problem, it can never be dissolved. On the contrary, the "problem" can do nothing but grow and proliferate in ever-increasing confusion. For it is an essential feature of thought that once the mind accepts a problem, then it is appropriate for the brain to keep on working until it finds a solution. This feature is indeed necessary for proper rational thinking. Thus, if a person were confronted by a real problem (e.g., the need to obtain food) and dropped it before it was adequately solved, the result could be disastrous. In any case, such a mode of operation would indicate an unhealthy flightiness or lack of seriousness. On the other hand, if the mind treats a paradox as if it were a real problem, then since the paradox has no "solution," the mind is caught in the paradox forever. Each apparent solution is found to be inadequate, and only leads on to new questions of a yet more muddled nature. Thus, a paradox which has taken root early in life (e.g., that arising out of a situation in which a child is made to feel a sense of inadequacy) may continue for the whole of a person's life, always changing in detail, growing more and more confused, but remaining the same in essence. And when the person becomes aware of the disorder in his mind, but describes this disorder as a problem, then this very step makes the activity around the paradox both more intense and more confused. Clearly, then, it is important to see the difference between a problem and a paradox, and to respond to each of these in a way that is appropriate to it.

This distinction is important, not only psychologically for the individual, but also for human relationships, and ultimately for establishing a proper order of society. Thus, one can see that it is wrong to describe a breakdown in human relationships as a problem. For example, it is now widely found that parents and children cannot communicate freely and easily. The paradox is that all concerned seem to understand their common humanity and mutual dependence, which imply the need to be open to each other, while nevertheless, each person feels that his own particular "needs" are being ignored or rejected by the other, so that he is "hurt" and reacts with a "defense mechanism" preventing him from really listening to what the other person means to say.

A similar paradox operates broadly throughout the whole of society, between different age groups, races, social classes, nations, etc. Thus, consider the prevailing tendency toward nationalism. People in each nation apparently understand the need for common human feeling and truthfulness in communications. Yet, when the nation is in danger, so strong is the reaction of fear and aggression that everyone is immediately ready to cease to treat the enemy as human (e.g., each side is ready to use bombs, killing children on the other side, when individually they would be horrified at the notion of child murder). And at home, they accept a censorship, which implies that they agree to take what is false as true, because they believe such self-deception to be necessary for the survival of the nation. Nationalism is thus seen to be rooted in a tremendous paradox. It therefore makes no sense to treat nationalism as a problem. The absurdity of such a procedure becomes evident if one puts forth the question of how one can be ready to annihilate children of another nationality and yet love children of one's own nationality. Such a question has no answer, and indeed the attempt to find an answer can only lead to further confusion. What is needed is that people be ready to give serious and sustained attention to a paradoxical pattern that has come to dominate their thinking and feeling.

Such paradoxical patterns go far beyond even questions of society and human relationships, and are indeed present in the whole of human thought and language. Since all that we do is shaped and formed by our modes of thinking and communication, these patterns based on paradoxes tend to bring about confusion in every phase of life.

Ultimately, this very pervasive set of patterns may be seen to grow out of a certain "root" paradox. To help bring out what this root paradox is, one may first consider the fact that ordinarily, thought has some external object or state of affairs for its content. For example, one may think of a chair, a house, a tree, a storm, the Earth in its orbit, etc. All of these share the characteristic that they are essentially independent of the process of thought which goes on in our minds, while at the same time this process of thought is essentially independent of the content (i.e., our thoughts are free to take this content or to leave it, and instead to range over some other content, which observation may indicate to be relevant).

Evidently, such relative independence of the mode of activity of thought from its content is appropriate when one is engaged in thinking about practical and technical subjects. However, when one begins to think about *himself*, and especially about his own thoughts and feelings, then if one observes carefully, he will find that this approach leads to a paradoxical pattern of activity. The paradox is that whereas one is treating his own

thinking and feeling as something separate from and independent of the thought that is thinking about them, it is evident
that in fact there is, and can be, no such separation and independence.

Take, for example, the case of the man who is susceptible to
flattery, because of a suppressed memory of a painful feeling of
inadequacy. This memory is itself part of his thinking, and vice
versa, all his subsequent thinking is conditioned by the memory,
in such a way that it will accept what is false as true, if to
do this seems to relieve the remembered sense of pain even
momentarily. So the thinking process is not separate from or
independent of its content. Therefore, when such a person puts
forth the problem of trying to control or overcome his tendency
to deceive himself, then he is caught in the "root paradox"; i.e.,
that the *activity* of his thought is controlled by the very thing that
it appears to be trying to control.

For ages, men have generally realized that thinking and feeling are commonly infected with greed, violence, self-deception,
fear, aggressiveness, and other forms of reaction that lead to
corruption and confusion. For the most part, however, all of this
has been regarded as a problem, and thus men have sought to
overcome or control the disorder in their own nature in countless ways. For example, all societies have instituted a set of
punishments, aimed at frightening people into right behavior,
along with a set of rewards aimed at enticing them toward the
same end. Because this has proved to be inadequate, men have
further set up systems of morals, and ethics, along with various
religious notions, with the hope that these would enable people,
of their own accord, to control their "wrong" or "evil" thoughts
and feelings. But this, too, has not really produced the desired
result. And indeed since the disorder in man's nature is the
outcome of a paradox, no attempt to treat it as a problem can
bring this disorder to an end. On the contrary, such attempts
will generally add to the confusion and thus, in the long run,
they may even produce more harm than good.

At present, mankind is faced with an almost explosive rate
of increase of the sort of difficulties that arise out of the attempt
to treat the disorder in his own thinking and feeling as if this
were a problem. Thus, it is now more urgent than ever that we
give attention not only to this outward state of affairs, but also
to the inward dullness and non-perceptiveness which allows

us to go on failing to notice the paradox in thinking and feeling in which the outward confusion has its deep origin. Each human being has to see that the very feelings and ideas which he is inclined to identify with his "innermost self" are involved in paradox, through and through. A mind caught in such paradox will inevitably fall into self-deception, aimed at the creation of illusions that appear to relieve the pain resulting from the attempt to go on with self-contradiction. Such a mind cannot possibly see the relationships of the individual and of society as they really are. And thus, the attempt to "solve one's own problems" and "to solve the problems of society" will in fact be found to propagate the existing confusion, rather than to help bring it to an end.

Of course, this does not mean that all working toward the establishment of order in the life of the individual and of society should now be dropped, in favor of concentration on the disorder in the mind that prevents the ending of our general difficulties. Rather, the inward work and the outward work go hand in hand. But it has to be kept in mind that through centuries of habit and conditioning, our prevailing tendency is now to suppose that "basically we ourselves are all right" and that our difficulties generally have outward causes, which can be treated as problems. And even when we do see that we are not in order inwardly, our habit is to suppose that we can point fairly definitely to what is wrong or lacking in ourselves, as if this were something different from or independent of the activity of thinking in which we formulate the "problem" of correcting what is in error.

As has been seen, however, the very process of thought with which we consider our personal and social "problems" is conditioned and controlled by the content which it seems to be considering so that, generally speaking, this thought can neither be free nor even really honest. What is called for, then, is a deep and intense awareness, going beyond the imagery and intellectual analysis of our confused process of thought, and capable of penetrating to the contradictory presuppositions and states of feeling in which the confusion originates. Such awareness implies that we be ready to apprehend the many paradoxes that reveal themselves in our daily lives, in our larger-scale social relationships, and ultimately in the thinking and feeling that appear to constitute the "innermost self" in each one of us.

In essence, therefore, what is needed is to go on with life in its wholeness and entirety, but with sustained, serious, careful attention to the fact that the mind, through centuries of conditioning, tends, for the most part, to be caught in paradoxes, and to mistake the resulting difficulties for problems.

5

THE OBSERVER AND THE
OBSERVED

Normally we don't see that our assumptions are affecting the
nature of our observations. But the assumptions affect the way
we see things, the way we experience them, and, consequently,
the things that we want to do. In a way, we are looking *through*
our assumptions; the assumptions could be said to be an
observer in a sense. The meaning of the word "observe" you
could get from defining "observation" as "gathering with the
eye," or "listening" as "gathering with the ear." That is, everything in the room you are in is gathered together and comes to
the pupil of the eye, the retina, and to the brain; or it may also
come through the ear. So the observer is what gathers: it selects
and gathers the relevant information and organizes it into some
meaning and picture. And that is what's done by the assumptions in thought. According to what you assume, you will collect
and gather certain information as important and put it together
in a certain way, in a certain structure.

Therefore, the assumptions are functioning as a kind of
observer. When we observe we forget that, and we are looking
without taking that into account. But this "observer" profoundly
affects what it is observing, and is also affected by what it is
observing – there is really very little separation between them. If
the emotions are what are being observed, then the "observing"
assumptions are profoundly affected by the emotions, and the
emotions are profoundly affected by the assumptions. On the
other hand, if you say the emotions are the observer, and are
determining the way things are organized, then the assumptions
will be the observed. Either way, the observed is profoundly
affected by the observer, and the observer by the observed –

they really are one cycle, one process. The separation between them is not very significant.

If, on the other hand, I observe a chair on the other side of the room, what's going on in me is not very much affected by the chair; and what's going on in the chair is not profoundly affected by me. We could say in that case that the observer is significantly different from the observed. But when looking at your emotions or looking at your thoughts, that cannot be the case. Similarly, when looking at society or looking at another person, what you see depends on your assumptions, and you will get an emotional reaction from that person which enters you and affects the way you see.

Therefore, at a certain stage the distinction between the observer and the observed cannot be maintained, or as Krishnamurti used to say, the observer *is* the observed. If you don't put the two together, the observer and the observed – if you don't put the assumptions together with the emotions – then the whole thing will be wrong. If I say I am going to look into my mind but I don't consider my assumptions, then the picture is wrong *because the assumptions are looking*. That is a common problem of introspection. You say, "I am going to look at myself inwardly," but the assumptions are not looked at – the assumptions are looking.

You could imagine a television program on the observer and the observed. There would be one person who would be the observer, and the other would be the observed. They would go through all the motions, so that one was quite carefully looking at the other, and the other was somewhat uncomfortable being looked at. You would get a feeling that the observer was looking at the observed. That's just the sort of thing going on in the mind: thought is producing an image of an observer and an image of the observed, and it's attributing itself to a thinker who is producing the thought and doing the observing. It's also attributing its being to the observed at the same time, just as we do ordinarily with regard to the body.

Just as I can observe the room that I am in, I can observe my body. But I also know that I *am* my body, and I experience this in another way, through sensations. This experience is then reproduced inwardly, through imagination and fantasy, as the observer and the observed. And as with the body, this is felt to be reality, the reality of the self.

This is a suggestion as to how it may work – that thought has come to attribute itself to an image of an observer, a thinker. This gives it much greater authority, because it has then apparently come from a *being* who should know what to think. On the other hand, if it's just going mechanically, it might have no more significance than a computer. But if you imagined there was a little being inside the computer, this too would take on much greater authority.

Consider the case of a blind man and his stick. If he holds the stick tightly when he is tapping, he feels the stick is "me" – he feels that he contacts the world at the end of the stick. If he holds the stick loosely, the stick is not me, but my hand is me. But then he may think, "My hand is not me, 'I' want to move 'my' hand." Therefore, there is something further inside that is still me, which is moving my hand. He keeps going more and more inward, taking off more and more, and saying, "That's not me, that's not me – I am going to look at these things, they are not essential to 'me.' " And he may get the feeling of the internal organs, the sense of the muscles, and think, "They are not me – I am just looking somewhere inside." And he could go on, peeling off the layers of the onion until he got to the very essence, the center, which at some point would really be "me." At some point he would say, "There must be some essential innermost 'me' that sort of looks at everything." That's the way people are thinking – everybody feels that way.

I am suggesting, however, that thought is a system belonging to the whole culture and society, evolving over history, and it creates the image of an individual who is supposed to be the source of thought. It gives the sense of an individual who is perceived and experienced. This would be conducive to the next step, which is for thought to claim that it only tells you the way things are and then the individual inside decides what to do with the information – he chooses. This is the picture which emerged gradually; thought tells you the way things are, and then "you" choose how to act from that information.

You may look at this and try to reason and see what is wrong. You begin to doubt, saying, "Whatever is behind this is doubtful." But very often, the first questions you ask will contain the very presupposition that should be doubted. As an example, I may question some belief, but I may question it through what amounts to another belief. So you have to be sensitive to the whole of what you are doing. What happens is that it seems that there is a "doubter" who doubts. Somewhere "back in the back" is somebody who is observing what is wrong, *but he is not being observed*. The very "wrong" things which he should be looking at are in the one who is looking, because that is the safest place to hide them. Hide them in the looker, and the looker will never find them.

6

SUSPENSION, THE BODY, AND PROPRIOCEPTION

We are trying to get deeper, to the very essence of the whole process that is behind the self, or the observer. The general difficulty that one has – in both listening and looking – is that if there is listening through a "listener," then we are not listening. Some part of you steps back and listens to the rest. If there is listening without a listener, then that is similar to observing without an observer. Everybody can do that on certain occasions – you take an action, and you are not observing yourself while you are doing it. You just do it. But then on other occasions you find it hard to do this. So really we have come to the question of what is needed to go deeply into observation, so that you can look at yourself without a "looker," or listen to yourself, or other people, without a "listener."

The first point is, what are we going to look at or listen to in connection with this issue? Suppose we have aggression or resistance. If a person is aggressive, he first acts – he may act physically, or with words, or with gestures and expressions – in some way he acts. Now, he doesn't know that he is acting when he acts. He doesn't know he is being aggressive, he just thinks, "I am right," or, "I have been attacked, this is necessary." He doesn't feel it as aggression. Then at some point he may notice what is happening. He may think, "I am aggressive, I mustn't be aggressive." That suppresses the action, which means that you are still aggressive, *against yourself*. So it hasn't changed. The observer of aggression is pervaded with aggression. Therefore, nothing happens.

There is another action, which is neither to carry out the aggression, nor to turn it against yourself by suppressing it. Rather, you may *suspend* the activity, allowing it to reveal itself,

73

to flower, to unfold, and so you see the aggression and its actual structure inside of you. Movements are taking place inside of you – physical feelings – the heartbeat, the blood pressure, the way you breathe, the way your body feels tense; and also the kinds of thoughts that go along with these feelings. You can observe these things, be aware of them, and of their connection. Ordinarily all those feelings and bodily reactions are taken to be one thing, and the thoughts something else, unconnected. But as you become aware of the connection, it becomes more clear that they are not independent of one another.

The human race doesn't do a great deal of suspension of this sort. I think that it is a natural potential, but that we have not developed in such a way as to favor it very much. Our development has been more toward a kind of immediate impulsive response that is favorable to violence. For example, you may often be in a situation where you think that a violent reaction is going to pay. Or you may say, "Society says one ought not to be violent. I will try not to be violent." But meanwhile you continue the thoughts that are making you violent. Either way you don't get anywhere. Violence thus constantly tends to grow. It goes into the "program," into the memory. The more you are violent, the more you leave a program for violence; then it becomes more and more automatic. I think that is one major factor. There is also a hereditary factor, which is that we may have some tendency to respond with force where we should suspend. But even in the jungle, force is not called for all the time. In fact, mostly suspension is what is called for, and force only occasionally. To survive there, you really would have to learn suspension.

In the process of suspension, you may notice two things. First, that physical reactions are being produced by thought, and therefore are not as significant as they would be if they were not being produced by thought. The tremendously excited state of your body, which seems one of the reasons why you should do something, is no longer as significant as you had thought. Second, you can get direct evidence that the thoughts are affecting the feelings and the feelings are affecting the thoughts *without passing through "me."*

The ordinary picture is that the only connection between thoughts, feelings, and actions is the central entity who does it all and experiences it all. That is one idea of how everything is

74

connected up, and that is why the "central entity" is felt to be so important: everything goes through him. He is at their source, their center. But in fact you can get evidence that thoughts and feelings move as processes on their own; they are not being run by "me." They are not being produced by the me, and they are not being experienced by the me.

There is, however, some self-reference built into the whole system. There is what is called *proprioception*, or "self-perception." Physically, a person is aware immediately that he has moved a part of his body. If some outside force suddenly moved your arm, you could tell that that is different from having moved it yourself. The nerves are built so as to be able to know that. In this connection, there was a woman who suffered a stroke while she was asleep, and she woke up apparently being attacked by somebody. But when the light was turned on, she was hitting herself. Her sensory nerves had been damaged, but not the motor nerves; therefore she had no way of knowing she was hitting herself. Consequently she assumed that something else was hitting her, and the more she struggled against the "assailant," the more she was hitting herself. So there is proprioception in the body – the distinction between actions which originate in the body, and those which originate outside, is perceived as a functional difference. In this light, the notion that there is a self as a kind of center, the body as a center of activity, is natural. Animals obviously have it too, and they can make that distinction. We can therefore say that this notion of "I" cannot be entirely wrong, or it probably would never have arisen.

The question is: how does this natural, useful distinction turn into the contradictions of the ego? Something that was correct and useful has somehow developed in a way which has gone wrong. Thought lacks proprioception, and we have got to learn, somehow, to observe thought. In the case of observing the body, you can tell that observation is somehow taking place – *even when there is no sense of a distinct observer.*

Is it possible for thought similarly to observe itself, to see what it is doing, perhaps by awakening some other sense of what thought is, possibly through attention? In that way, thought may become proprioceptive. It will know what it is doing and it will not create a mess. If I didn't know what I was doing when I made an outward physical action, everything

ON DIALOGUE

would go wrong. And clearly, when thought doesn't know what it is doing, then such a mess arises. So let us look further – first at suspension, then at proprioception.

I want to emphasize again that with anger, violence, fear – with all those things, there can be suspension. If we suspend anger, then we are going to see that anger has certain thoughts and assumptions that keep it going. If you accept those assumptions, you will go on being angry. Or you could say, "I shouldn't be angry. I'm not angry, really." Then you would lose awareness of being angry while you remain angry. That would be suppressing awareness. You would still be violent. What is called for is not suppressing the awareness of anger, nor suppressing nor carrying out its manifestations, but rather, suspending them in the middle at sort of an unstable point – as on a knife-edge – so that you can look at the whole process. That is what is called for.

So the first point is: is it possible to suspend the action without suppressing it? If you find it is not possible, *then you observe the process of suppression without suppressing the suppression* – without telling yourself you're not suppressing. In addition, you may find that there is an observer who is suspending the action. Then you observe the suspension – you observe that there is an *effort* to suspend the action. The point is, there is no formula for this. I am not suggesting a formula or a prescription, but a point of departure for an inquiry. We cannot tell exactly where it is going to lead. You will perhaps find that you can't stop this thing rolling. But then you will find that there is some other thing you are doing, and at a certain stage somehow *that* can be suspended. At that point you will find you can look.

Another approach could be that you get an outburst of anger and it cools down. It simmers down, but it's still there. You put it in abeyance because something more important comes up, but the anger is still there, ready to come up. You can then call it up *on purpose* by trying to find the words that express the reason for being angry. You can go over the thoughts that actually come to you. Then when you have a thought that carries great force – somebody has frightened you or hurt you, and you say, "I'm hurt" – watch what happens. This is much harder than watching a thought which carries lesser force.

What is behind the hurt is a previous thought which says, "I'm not hurt, I'm feeling pretty good." It all depends on certain kinds of things: "My friends must think of me in a certain way; this must be this way (and so on), and then I can feel fairly good." That's in the background. It's not conscious, but it's there. And then somebody says, "You're an idiot. You're no good at all." This new thought comes in which produces an opposite, bad feeling, and there's a shock. At first you don't know what it is. Watch that. The content of the thought behind it is, "What in the world has happened?" You'll begin to see that this is very habitual. Your explanation is that you've been hurt. That explanation is duly displayed as pain. Since it's supremely important, the pain is very great. That all happens in a flash – the machinery has been set up, and it explodes. If you can't watch it in the moment that it actually happens, you can watch it afterwards – you can recall it. Recall it by the words: go over the words which hurt you, and see what happened.

You will find that the words which first hurt you will hurt you again. You can see how that comes about. You will find all sorts of subsidiary thoughts like, "I trusted him and he betrayed me." Or, "I gave him everything and look what he does." There are a million such thoughts. The thing to do is to find the words which express what's going on, and see what those words do – not for the purpose of finding the content of the words, but for the purpose of seeing what they *do*. There is a difference between thinking *about* the hurt, and *thinking the hurt*. Thinking *about* the hurt is saying that the hurt is "out there," and I form abstractions about it, like a table. Therefore, I'm not doing anything, because the hurt isn't like a table – it's *me*. The other way is to *think the hurt*, which is to go through the thought and let it produce whatever it's going to do, which means to let it stand in the body and in consciousness without being suppressed and without being carried out. Suspend the activity in both directions, and just simply let it reveal itself, and see it.

Now, in order to get a clearer picture of the meaning of proprioception, I'll first discuss coherence, incoherence, and the tacit process of thought. Incoherence means that your intentions and your results do not agree. Your action is not in agreement with what you expect. You have contradiction, confusion, and you have self-deception in order to cover it up. Some incoherence is inevitable, because knowledge is not perfect. All knowledge is limited, because it is an abstraction from the whole. It consists only of what you have learned up to this point. As knowledge is always limited in this way, it is going to have the possibility of being incoherent. The incoherence shows up when knowledge is applied, when you act according to knowledge. Or it can show up when you try to work something out through knowledge. If your attitude is a proper one, you say, "Okay. I acknowledge the incoherence. I will let go of my past knowledge. Let me find out." You find out what is wrong and change it. But if you defend that knowledge, you are off on a wrong track. There is no reason to defend knowledge, but people are caught up all the time in defending it.

On the other hand, we sense coherence as order, beauty, harmony. But if somebody only looks at order, beauty, and harmony, he could easily start fooling himself and say that everything is working nicely – it's all orderly, harmonious, and beautiful. So we need the "negative" sense of incoherence – *which is the road to coherence*. If a person is sensitive to incoherence, he begins acknowledging it, and then finding out what its source is. Coherence is evidently of tremendous value to us. It has to be, because incoherent functioning is really very dangerous. In addition, we are built so that we somehow appreciate coherence. It is part of life. If your life is totally incoherent, you might feel that it is hardly worthwhile. So we have a sense of value built in, but our values have become mixed up. As thought developed over the ages, it produced incoherent values which muddle us. For instance, if we have a desire for coherence we can go about it wrongly and simply try to *impose* coherence, rather than discovering the incoherence and dropping it. This is a kind of violence, and therefore a further extension of incoherence.

I suggest that the movement toward coherence is innate, but our thought has muddled it. A highly incoherent response is on the program in memory. We don't know how to get at it or what it means – and it has become more and more entangled as time has gone on. Coherence includes the entire process of the mind – which includes the tacit processes of thought. Therefore, any change that really counts has to take place in the tacit, concrete process of thought itself. It cannot take place only in abstract thought.

This tacit, concrete process is *actual* knowledge, and it may be coherent or not. In the case of riding a bicycle, if you don't know how to ride, then the knowledge isn't right – the tacit knowledge is not coherent in the context of trying to ride the bike, and you don't get the intended result. The incoherence becomes clear – you fall when you want to ride. Physically, tacit knowledge is where the action is coming from. And physical change depends on changing the tacit response.

Therefore, changing the abstract thought is one step, but unless it also changes the way the body responds, it won't be enough. Someone could say, "You're not doing it right. You're turning in the wrong direction. You should turn to the direction you're falling, but your instinct is making you turn the other way." All of that would help, but eventually it has to come into the tacit. You need the tacit knowledge *which you get by actually riding*, and then you are sort of correcting the previous knowledge. There is a *movement* in that tacit knowledge, which is that it is exploring possibilities. When tacit knowledge moves and finds a result in the direction you have been aiming for, it then continues – it goes in that direction some more. That's the way it learns, until you finally find yourself riding the bicycle. You may be guided by the abstract map, but you need the tacit knowledge as well.

The question is: can we do this in thought as well as in bicycle riding? I am proposing that thought – to think – is actually a tacit process more subtle than riding the bicycle. The concrete process of thinking is very tacit. At the actual level where thinking emerges in the tacit process, it is a movement. In principle, that movement could be self-aware. I suggest that there is a possibility for self-awareness of thought – that the concrete, real process of the movement of thought could be self-aware, without bringing in a "self" who is aware of it.

"Proprioception" is a technical term – you could also say "self-perception of thought," "self-awareness of thought," or "thought is aware of itself in action." Whatever terms we use, I am saying: thought should be able to perceive its own movement, be aware of its own movement. In the process of thought there should be the awareness of that *movement*, of the *intention* to think, and of the *result* which that thinking produces. By being more attentive, we can be aware of how thought produces a result outside ourselves. And then maybe we could also be attentive to the results it produces within ourselves. Perhaps we could even be immediately aware of how it affects perception.

If you move your body, you are aware immediately that you have moved it. It is not a kind of conscious cognizance, but rather it's almost unconscious. You know that you have moved it, that something else has not moved it. There is an awareness between your *impulse* to act and the act itself.

Physically when you make a move, you have to know immediately what the result is, without thought, without thinking, so that there is no time-lag in the feedback. If it takes a lot of time it won't work. This is essential for survival. Thus, proprioception is built into the physical movements of the body. And it can be improved – athletes and dancers learn to make it better – but it is not perfect in anybody, because for many of your movements you are not aware of what you are doing. But still it is there.

What about thought? You have the *impulse* to think. Then thought occurs, and all sorts of things happen – "felts" occur, the body gets tense, and so on. But if you don't see the connection, it would be like the woman who thought someone else was hitting her. She did something, and thought she didn't do it – that somebody else did it. To get that wrong is all the difference in the world. As an example, suppose you see someone you don't like, and begin to think, "What a terrible person he is. I can't stomach him." That thought might be almost automatic – you don't even put it in words. But you could get a pain in the stomach. You might then say, "Something is wrong with my stomach." Your heart-rate may change, or other things may happen. Emotions may arise as you think of that person who hurt you and didn't have any regard for you. You say, "Well, I have deep gut feelings about this, which must really be valid." *That's a failure of proprioception in thought.*

In this connection, there is a device that can measure the resistance of the skin, which shows changes according to your emotional state. If somebody says something to you causing you to react, two or three seconds later a needle jerks – it takes that time for the impulse to work its way down from the brain through the nervous system. You may not even notice you had some sort of emotional reaction – although if you had a strong one you will notice it – but it affects you either way. If it gets strong enough to be noticed you will say, "I had a gut feeling."

Now, the person said something to you two or three seconds ago, but you don't see the connection. You don't connect it, and you say, "There is a deep gut feeling, which is a sign that I'm justified in being angry." You use the feeling to justify the anger, and you say, "Here is an independent gut feeling, which shows that I'm perceiving something. It shows that my anger is *right*." Then those thoughts arouse more feeling, and so on and on. Without proprioception, you cannot get this right.

Later, you can figure it out and say, "I can see that it was my thought that did it." But by that time, everything is stirred up and you can't get it straight. Whereas if you had proprioception of thought, you would immediately say, "Well, I had the impulse to think, I thought something, and then came that feeling. It was caused in that way, and therefore that is all it means." But if you get the feeling that it does not come from a thought, then it will tacitly be taken to mean a direct perception of reality.

I think that there is a natural potential for spontaneous proprioception of thought. The mind may have proprioception built in, the same way that the body has – in the tacit process there is self-awareness. *That may be the very nature of mind.* But it is very subtle. It has been inhibited; otherwise you would say, "Okay, there's a thought that builds up an image that's frightening, or uncomfortable. But since it's just an image, it's not very important." Instead you say, "I mustn't think of that." Or you don't even consider what's happening – you just start moving away. You can't keep your mind on it. It jumps, attention goes to something else, or you forget. You constantly forget, getting senses of anesthesia or dullness. The brain is producing all that to prevent you from getting into that painful thought – it is trying to protect you from what it regards as something very bad.

The essential thing is that the body process is a movement, beginning with an impulse and going on to a result, and *you sense it as it develops.* Now thought is also a movement – if it is a process, it is also a movement. But thought doesn't treat itself as a movement. It treats itself as truth – as just being there, telling you the way things are. In principle the movement of thought could be self-aware, except that all this muddle is going on, so it can't work. It's like the lights of Las Vegas, which prevent you from seeing the universe. You might think that those lights are the most important thing in the world, because they are so powerful and they fill your consciousness. But something very subtle may be far more important.

In this respect, there is a further way we can look at this which gives some insight: that is to look at thought as a system of *reflexes*. A reflex means that when a certain thing happens, something else happens automatically. We have a lot of reflexes, and they can be conditioned. For instance, dogs have a reflex that makes them salivate when they see food. Pavlov did an experiment where he rang a bell while showing food to a dog. He did this many times, and after a while the dog would salivate without seeing food, just from hearing the bell. That is the basic form of conditioning – to repeat something quite often. You can see the conditioning of reflexes all the time – a great deal of our routine learning consists in establishing conditioned reflexes. When you learn to drive a car, you are trying to condition your reflexes so that they will be appropriate.

Elementary thoughts may take the form of a series of reflexes. If somebody asks you your name, you have an immediate answer. It's a reflex. With a more difficult question there's a way the mind searches in the memory for answers. A "searching reflex" is set up – the mind searches the memory, finds an answer that may seem to fit, and then that answer comes out and you can see whether it fits or not. I suggest that this whole system is a set of reflexes – that thought is a very subtle set of reflexes which is potentially unlimited; you can add more and more, and you can modify your reflexes. Even the whole logical process, once it's committed to memory, becomes a set of reflexes. And that's what I want to call "thought" – which includes the emotions, the bodily state, the physical reaction, and everything else.

Thought, then, is part of a material process. It goes on in the brain, the nervous system, the whole body – it's all one system. Thought can be conveyed by material processes such as radio waves, television, or writing. In talking, sound goes out and conveys thought. Within the body, thought is conveyed by nervous system signals; there is a code of some sort which we don't know too well. I'm saying that thought is a material process – it has reflexes that just go on by themselves. If you have an insight or perception that this is true, then this will actually affect you. An insight or perception of truth may deeply affect the material process, which includes all the reflexes. But if we have merely intellectual or inferential knowledge of what is going on, then it doesn't touch this process deeply.

Matter may be infinitely subtle. Science doesn't know all about it, and probably never will. But matter is not just mechanical. Therefore, it could respond to perception in very deep and subtle ways which may be beyond what science could even trace; there could be a change. That's the notion: that insight or perception will affect the whole thing. It not only affects the inferential understanding, but it also affects the chemical level, the tacit level – everything.

The point is that we have the possibility of insight. Suppose we ask ourselves, "Do we have it as an insight that thought is a material process, or that thought always participates in perception?" If we have that insight, then that may remove some of the barriers. But our whole set of reflexes, our tacit knowledge, is against that. It says, "Thought is not a material process." Our first reflex is: "Thought is far beyond matter, or separated from matter somehow. It has some spiritual truth or significance." This notion has been conditioned into us as a reflex.

Now, however, we're saying that thought is a material process and thought participates – which means the notion that thought is only telling you what things are is not really a serious option. If that comes as an insight, *or if you get the insight that thought is not proprioceptive but requires proprioception,* then that could begin to touch the synapses in the brain which hold those reflexes.

7

PARTICIPATORY THOUGHT
AND THE UNLIMITED

In early human cultures, and to some extent even now, there has existed what has been called "participatory thought." People in such cultures felt that they were participating in some of the things that they saw – that everything in the world was participating, and that the spirit of things was all one. Eskimos, for instance, apparently had a belief that there were many, many seals, but that each one was a manifestation of the *one* seal – the spirit of the seal. That is, the one seal was manifesting as the many. Therefore, they could pray to this spirit of the seal to manifest so they could have something to eat. I think that some American Indians looked at the buffalo in that way. Such people felt that they were participating in nature, and in some way they were keenly aware of the participation of their thought.

We might now say, "That's a silly way to look at it – it's obviously many different seals." We've developed a more objective kind of thought which says, "We want to have a thought about something where we don't participate, where we think about it and know just what it is." But this modern way is a different way of thought. To the Eskimos it looks one way, and to us it looks another way.

Another way to illustrate participatory thought is to imagine that we are talking together. I see you, and I hear you; these are very different experiences. But my actual experience is that the person I see *is* the person I hear – they are one and the same. It is a *way of thought* that puts them together. Likewise you could say, "The breath that is going on in me is the spirit which is the Great Spirit or the universal spirit. And the heart, the lungs, the stomach are participating in the whole thing."

That would be very similar to the way the participatory cultures thought.

Participatory thought is a different way of perceiving and thinking, and that is the way we were for more or less a million years. In the last five thousand years we have turned it around, and our present language says, "That's all nonsense. We won't pay attention to that at all." This kind of thought, which we largely favor nowadays, has been called "literal thought."

Literal thought aims at being a reflection of reality *as it is* – it claims just to tell you the way things are. We tend to say that's the best kind of thought. Technical thought, for instance, aims to be literal. Such thought intends to be unambiguous; it may not succeed, but it aims that way – to know something as exactly what it is. Owen Barfield has compared such literal thought to idol worship. If you make an idol, it may stand in at first for some force which is greater than itself, or for some spiritual energy. But gradually the idol is taken to be *it* – literally; and therefore you give supreme value to that object. We could say that in a way we are worshiping our words and our thoughts, insofar as they claim to be descriptions or statements about reality *just as it is*. In fact, they cannot do that – we are giving them too high a value. They can cover some of reality, but they don't cover "all."

Cultures that used a great deal of participatory thought probably also used literal thought for practical activities, but the things that deeply mattered to them mostly involved participatory thought. Tribes would have a totem – certain animals with which they were identified – and say, "The tribe and the totem – we are identical." The thought is that they and the totem are participating together in some sort of energy or spirit. Or they may even say that all of existence is participating in a universal spirit or matter. Just as I say that the person I hear is the person I see, so they say the totem is the tribe. You contact the tribe through the totem, or contact the totem through a person, or through the people as a whole.

It is very interesting to put yourself in that place, to try to think that way. I suggest that we are constantly doing participatory thought anyway, that it has never gone away. An example would be that when my country is attacked, *I* am attacked. We are then doing exactly that kind of thought. We say, "I am my country. When you cross that boundary, you have hit *me*." We do a great deal of that kind of thought, but we claim we are not doing it. Literal thought claims we are not doing it at all. Therefore, it is incoherent. Explicitly we have given supreme value to literal thought, while in fact we are also tacitly giving supreme value to participatory thought. So it's all very muddled. Literal thought took over in conscious awareness and made technology possible, and in many ways it was of tremendous advantage to do that. At the same time, participatory thought somehow went into the shade; it got eclipsed, but it remained underground.

Now what does this word "participation" mean? It really has two meanings. The earliest meaning was, "to partake *of*," as you partake of food – people all eating from the common bowl, partaking of bread or whatever it is. Symbolically, or even actually, to these early people it meant partaking of the *source*. They felt that the totem and they themselves partook of this energy; this created a sense of oneness. In western culture, this meaning persisted until the Middle Ages. The second meaning is "to partake *in*," to make your contribution. In modern times this has become the major meaning. It means that you are accepted, you are being taken into the whole. You can't take part in something unless that thing in some sense accepts your participation. Taken together, these ways of thinking do not create a separation of object and subject. As implicit thought, this would create a sense or feeling of being together – *that boundaries are not really separations*, but that they are there for descriptive purposes.

In the Middle Ages, Thomas Aquinas used the idea of participation constantly. He would say that the subject of the sentence participates in the object. He would also say that the light we see on the earth participates in the sun. The light is there in the pure quality in the sun, and we are partaking of it here. That's a way of thinking which has been common over a tremendous part of our human development, and we should really get the flavor of it. That way of thinking would not lead anybody to plunder the planet. We are partaking of the planet, and to plunder it would be absurd. Deep down in the unconscious such thinking must be part of us all, because the human race has had maybe a million years of that way of thinking, and a comparatively short time in which literal thought has been dominant.

Participatory thought sees that everything partakes of everything. It sees that its own *being* partakes of the earth – it does not have an independent being. It's the same as to say we are nourished by the earth. Suppose we consider food – you partake of food, literally. That food, which looks like a separate object, becomes you. *Where* does it become you? *How* can it become you? At what stage? Where do you draw the line? As you can see, something is wrong with looking at the food as literally a separate object. Such literal thought tends to fragment, while the participatory thought tends to bring things together.

But participatory thought has some aspects that are very inadequate, or even dangerous. For example, in some tribes, the word for "human being" was the same as the word for a member of that tribe. When they met another tribe, the very word suggested that the other tribe was not human. They might have known in some sense they were, but the power of such words is enormous. Therefore, that tribe may not have been able to include other tribes in their "participation"; it would break down at that point, and they would begin fragmentary thinking.

Another example would be the beer cellars in the time of Hitler's Germany. People would sit in the beer cellars and sing, with great participation and comradeship, "We're all friends together, we're going to go out and conquer the world and it will all be wonderful." But when it came to the action, it wasn't so wonderful. So you can see that this notion of participatory thought is not necessarily a formula for perfect happiness.

Half a million years ago people didn't really need much literal thought. They lived in small groups of hunter-gatherers; they all knew one another, and developed literal thought only for simple technical purposes. But then came the agricultural revolution, and larger societies developed. These societies needed much more organization and order and technology, and they had to use much more literal thought. They organized society by saying, "You belong here, you do this, you do that." *They began, therefore, to treat everything as a separate object, including other people.* They used people as means to an end. The further civilization went, the more these societies went into this area of using thought as a means to an end.

Such thought then entered into the relationship between countries. Each country treated the other country as an object, which was to be controlled, or fought over, or defeated. There was a constant spread of the practical, technical form of thought into more and more areas. Participation itself became fragmentary, and receded; it withdrew into a limited area, which got more limited all the time. Perhaps people had it in the family or in certain rituals – in the sense of the city, or the country, or the religion or God – but more and more things were going on which were "worldly," as they said.

However, participation is absolutely necessary if anything is to be done collectively. But currently it isn't working right, because it's muddled up with literal thought. Therefore, we've got to understand the distinction between participatory thought and literal thought. How to draw that distinction is not clear, because to some extent we need literal thought even internally, psychologically. And to some extent we need the participatory thought outwardly. So we can't draw the line all that clearly – we have to learn about this. I think we need to understand more deeply why we're getting into this trouble.

Consider the organization of any sort of contemporary bureaucracy or hierarchy. In such an organization, people are treated as objects: they have to do *this* and *this* and *this*, and be related in *that* way. Literal thought knows the person by his function – he *is* whatever you call him – a worker, a banker, this or that. That sets up the social hierarchy – people are isolated from each other, and the participation is very limited.

So you once again have this same problem – that you have created the *object*. In such a view, the world is made of objects, literally. We treat other people as objects, and eventually you must treat yourself as an object, saying, "I must fit in here, and I must do this and be that and become better," or whatever. *But "society" is not an objective reality – period. It is a reality created by all the people through their consciousness.* It has some "objective" features you can point to once people have created it, particularly because there are so many taking part – it is statistical. The same thing happens in physics. If you try to measure one atom exactly, you can't do it – it participates. But if you take a statistical array of atoms, you can get an average that is objective. It comes out the same no matter who does it, or when. The average comes out, but the individual atom does not. And in society you can also get average behaviors, which are often predictable. But they are not very significant, compared with the thing that really moves us and makes the society come into being. Individually and collectively – together – we have a *consciousness* which creates this society, and sustains it with thought, intellect, feeling, and so on.

Similarly, in a dialogue group you could say that everybody is different – "I am here, you are there, you know this, I know that," and so on. But we could also say that participation is taking place, which means everybody is partaking of whatever is going on, and also maybe making a contribution. Even if you don't make a visible contribution, you're still partaking, and taking part in some way. All the thoughts, feelings, views, opinions come in, and they are growing in us, even as we think we are resisting them. We are particularly affected by the thought, "That's his view, and this is mine" – which is false. *All the views are just thought.* Wherever thought is, it is just thought – it is all one. It's similar to the Eskimos saying, "It's all one seal," only this seems even more so. Here we have an example where that kind of participatory view really works. Thought is all one, manifesting in all sorts of places and with all sorts of specific content. So the spirit of a dialogue is important in facing this question of literal and participatory thought, even though we realize that we are going in a direction which a very large part of the culture doesn't agree with at all.

But as long as we stick only to this literal thought, there is no room in it for participation. We think only of external mechanical relationships. We think the self is there as an object, and that everything comes from this self. I would propose, however, that in true participation, thought may establish distinctions, but there is participation *between* those distinctions – between people, between thought and feeling, between anything. I will say: ultimately the nature of all the world is that it is all mutual participation – everything is everything. That is what was meant in my book, *Wholeness and the Implicate Order*. It's another way of looking at things – to say everything "enfolds" everything. Ultimately, the ground of everything is the *en-folded*, and the *un-folded* is just a display, or a show of the enfolded.

I think one of the fundamental mistakes of the human race has been to say that when you have finished with a thought, it's gone. But it hasn't gone – it has "folded back" into the rest of consciousness. You don't know it's there any more, but it is still there; it may unfold again, or unfold in another form. So there's a constant process of unfolding from the background of consciousness into the foreground, and then back again. There could also be feelings that unfold as thoughts. And then the thoughts go back and give rise to more feelings, and movements of the body, and so on. It's a constant process. Perhaps we could say that it never "began" and will never end, because it goes back into nature, all the way back, as far as you can go. The human race, and all living species, have "unfolded" from the environment.

In this connection, I want to discuss three dimensions of the human being. One is the *individual*, just by himself. The individual body is in certain ways separate from others – although not totally, because it merges with air and light and food. There is no place where the body really ends – its boundary is relative. We can't say that when an oxygen molecule comes into the body, it suddenly becomes alive, and that when it leaves as carbon dioxide it's dead. We must say that there is really no sharp end to the body. And perhaps we can't even say where life begins and ends, but rather that the body is a sort of "focus" of life at a certain place. Nonetheless, each individual has peculiar features – physical features, due to heredity, DNA, and the rest; and certain mental features: experiences, background, capacities, and so on. In addition, he has a self-image, by which he tries to identify himself.

Then we have the *collective* dimension of the human being, where we have a considerable number of people – a society and a culture. That has a qualitatively new feature: it has great power, both potentially and actually. In dialogue we discuss how to bring that power to some sort of coherence and order.

And then there's a third dimension – the *cosmic* dimension, which is the sphere of man's immersion in nature, the cosmology of science and of religion. Human beings have always had that in mind, from the most ancient, prehistoric times. Nature is sensed as something beyond the individual or society. In the early days, as we have said, there was animism – people felt that everything was animate, that it had a spirit, and they were participating in all that. But as people moved away from nature into cities and onto farms (even the farm is quite far from wild nature), they began to feel the need for the cosmic, and they may have introduced various ways of trying to fulfill that need. In those very early times there was art, which probably had a sort of cosmic connection, and there followed notions of religion and philosophy – attempting to make a connection that way.

That has persisted, but large numbers of people no longer believe in the assumptions of religion. Religion has left us, we have moved very far away from nature, and philosophy has become confused. In modern society, science attempts to connect us to the cosmos to some extent; but it is limited, and most people can't understand it all that well anyway. Therefore, the connection to the cosmic dimension seems to be rather lost. But I think that people want to come back into that cosmic dimension. It is an essential dimension of the human being, along with the individual and the collective dimensions.

We could say that the bond of our connection to the cosmos has been broken. It has been suggested in various pieces of literature that we are at the "end of nature." Originally we thought of nature as vast, beyond that which human beings could do anything about. But now we can see that we are at the point of being able to destroy it. Tribal cultures have said, "The earth is our mother – we have to take care of the mother"; now people say, "No, that's not how it is. We've got to exploit the earth." And this change of our relationship with nature – this ending of the bond with nature – has another effect. People used to say, "Well, I know things are pretty bad here, but nature is 'out there,' and it's still okay." Now, however, the luxury of that view is gone. We can no longer rely on nature as being limitless.

Once people realize that, it makes a very big psychological change. It's like somebody saying, "You can't count on your mother any more. You're on your own." That's the sort of situation we're in – whether nature survives or not may well depend on us. Thus, there is a new orientation implied there: that we are really responsible for all of this planet. The question is then: what is the ground of that? *What are we?*

What is our nature? From what inner resources can we draw, to be that responsible? What is our being that would allow us to be responsible? What would be the ground of that possibility? We have not generally thought of ourselves as that sort of being. It's like somebody who grows up thinking mother or father will take care of him. Then he sees, "Well, now it's changed. It's the other way around."

Some people think we can survive by organizing nature, by finding species of trees and plants that can live despite the pollution – producing new species through genetic engineering, or some other means. They think that we could industrialize our world so much that nature itself is industrialized – we might even call it the "nature industry." We now have the entertainment industry, and practically have a culture industry and an education industry; similarly, we could have the nature industry. We could try simultaneously to conserve nature and to make it profitable. Maybe technology could open that up; we can't know. It looks a little dubious, but perhaps it is possible. But then, where would that leave us? What kind of a life would that be? That would be "participatory," but not a kind of participation that seems good.

We are playing a bigger and bigger part in this whole thing, and we have got to take this into account. We have to consider that nature has an almost religious significance in our psyche – that taking this new attitude has a very great implication for the human being. So, part of the cosmic dimension is man's attitude toward nature. But there is something beyond even that – not merely the cosmos as we see it through the telescope or looking out at the night sky. I think there is a ground beyond that. I want to suggest that there is something beyond limit, something not finite.

Living in ordinary society, you may give priority to money, to your country, or to whatever else you may be doing. You have all sorts of things to which you could give priority, and different people do it differently. However, if you give first priority to only those things, then you cannot be giving it to what may be *unlimited*. Your brain is effectively saying that there isn't any such thing as the unlimited. But in a participatory view, the suggestion is that we have the unlimited as the ground of everything – that our *true being* is unlimited. Then the question arises – is there a possibility of consciousness actually contacting the true being? I think everybody knows what the question means. People have gone into it in many, many ways over the ages.

However, there seems to be something in the structure of thought in civilization which tends to claim that we are going to get to know *everything*, and control it all. But we should ask: is it in the nature of thought to be able to know everything – since thought is abstraction, which inherently implies limitation? Or put differently: is the whole field of thought – experience, knowledge, tacit thought – *is that field limited*? A great deal of our culture would say that it is not limited. The assumption is that no matter what happens, by approaching it through thought, knowledge, and skill of application, we can deal with it. Now, I say that this assumption will go into implicit, tacit thought – and then it means that no matter what happens, *you're going to think*. That assumption is very dynamically active – it's a universal assumption, an assumption about "all." It is extremely powerful, with extremely great value, and it will "work." It will tend to take precedence over almost anything. You will find, therefore, that you are automatically thinking about everything, because the assumption is at work that thinking is not only possible, and at least potentially relevant, *but that it's the only way*.

I am proposing, however, that the field of thought is limited. I am also suggesting that there is the "unlimited," which contains the limited. This "unlimited" is not just in the direction of going to greater and greater distances out to the end of the universe; but much more importantly, it is also going into more and more subtlety. As we've seen, however, our attention tends to be limited by the tacit thoughts as to what has value, what's worth being attended to. If you don't attend to something, then you don't perceive it – it doesn't exist as far as you're concerned. But attention is not *intrinsically* restricted – it could widen out and go into any form. It may well be that attention is, as it were, a kind of relation between the limited and the unlimited – at least potentially so. There may be a limited kind of attention, such as concentration, as well as an unlimited kind – the fundamental kind. Through such attention, we could move into more and more subtle levels of the implicate order – the more general levels of the whole process. At these general levels, consciousness in one person differs very little from consciousness in another. Those implicit, tacit thoughts that are the foundation of consciousness are shared by all.

It may be that one of the brain's functions could be to be sensitive to more and more subtle levels of being; the brain could then function more as an antenna to pick up such levels, rather than as something that would be only the "initiator" of action. As long as the brain is following only its own internal goals, then it will be occupied; and that's necessary in certain contexts. But if we consider that it's also necessary to reach or contact the unlimited, then there must be a silence – a lack of occupation.

I think that most of our experience is in the implicate order, but we have been learning through society not to value it; we have learned to put the main value on the explicate, outward order, which is useful for the purposes we generally have in mind – making a living and doing this and that. So we need to establish a place somewhere, where we can have leisure, as it were, to go into this. The word *leisure* has a root meaning "emptiness" – an empty space of some sort – an empty space of time or place, where there is nothing occupying you. You might begin by looking at nature, where there are minimal distractions. Then, if a group of people really trusted each other and had a right spirit of fellowship, something like that may arise in a dialogue.

If you had a considerable number of people who really could see through this, they would have an effect immensely beyond any one person. We don't really know how much impact this will have, but there are real possibilities. There is currently a great deal of cynicism and pessimism about the human race, which has its point. But this cynicism can easily become false. The human race has great possibilities, which are being destroyed by some rather trivial things.

Getting to the root of all this belongs to all of mankind: we have something which can, potentially, produce a revolution. It depends on the intensity and the energy. It seems that the key is that we are going to have to pay attention to this whole thing. However, we may pay attention to something quite well, but then everything seems to go to pieces when there is trouble. At that point, instead of condemning ourselves, we've got to find out how that distraction was part of the same process. Studying the distractions is part of the process of learning; it is crucial to see these things in the presence of distractions, as well as in a quiet place. I think that when you get strong enough, as it were, that you can stand firm in a distracting environment, then you're strong enough to begin to look at the infinite – but the infinite

94

might be so powerful that its effects would distract you if you looked at it too quickly.

I think, then, that there is the possibility of the transformation of consciousness, both individually and collectively. It's important that it happen together – it's got to be both. And therefore this whole question – of communication and the ability to dialogue, the ability to participate in communication – is crucial.

BIBLIOGRAPHY

Barfield, Owen (1965) *Saving the Appearances*, New York: Harcourt, Brace and World.
Bohm, David (1980) *Wholeness and the Implicate Order*, London: Routledge.
—— (1987) *Unfolding Meaning*, London: Routledge.
—— (1994) *Thought as a System*, London: Routledge.
—— (1996) *Ojai Seminar Transcripts, 1986–1989*, Ann Arbor: University Microfilms International.
—— and Edwards, Mark (1991) *Changing Consciousness*, San Francisco: Harper San Francisco.
—— and Krishnamurti, J. (1985) *The Ending of Time*, San Francisco: Harper and Row.
de Mare, Patrick, Piper, Robin, and Thompson, Sheila (1991) *Koinonia*, London: Karnac.
Krishnamurti, Jiddu (1969) *Freedom from the Known*, New York: Harper and Row.
—— (1979) *The Wholeness of Life*, San Francisco: Harper and Row.
Polanyi, Michael (1966) *The Tacit Dimension*, New York: Garden City.

INDEX